SEEKER OF THE LIGHT

A spiritual guide to peace, joy and fulfilment

FIONA SUTTON

ACKNOWLEDGEMENTS

My deepest and sincerest gratitude goes to all those people who have supported me in writing this book. I am indebted to family and friends for their assistance in editing the book and their honest feedback.

I owe my reiki teacher, Helen Courtney, a big thank you, for her massive support and encouragement on my spiritual path, empowering me to achieve things I never thought possible. You are a true earth angel, and I am so proud to be your student.

I am so grateful to my two children for being the inspiration for writing this book. My desire to pass on the knowledge I have acquired, to create a happy and fulfilling life, lit a flame inside me, providing the motivation and courage to start writing. I am also indebted to my husband for his unfailing support; made more notable by the fact that he does not share my spiritual beliefs.

A sincere and heartfelt thank you must also go to all the lightworkers out there, who are doing their utmost every day to create a better and more harmonious world. Your books, videos and daily positive contributions on facebook, helped open my heart and mind, facilitating a different way of viewing reality and helping me to connect to my true and authentic self.

Last but not least, this book would never have been born if it wasn't for the miracles and other-worldly experiences that have occurred so frequently in my life. I felt divinely inspired to write this book, and the whole experience has been incredibly joyful. It seemed that I was being guided every step of the way, so to the Universe there is only one thing left to say, "Thank you, Thank you, Thank you."

Deep within your soul is a door that

Opens into a world of wonder.

Open the door

And let the magic in.

Contents

FOREWORD

Reality is merely an illusion, albeit a very persistent one.

Albert Einstein

For 26 years I shared my life with a very special horse; a horse that taught me how joyful and harmonious a union can be between horse and human. That horse gave me the best of her heart and soul. Her gifts to me were too many to mention, but she was saving the best for last. For when the time came to leave her physical body, the miracles that were gifted to me, awakened me to a completely different reality, and a pathway opened up that would lead me to a much more purposeful, happier and fulfilling life.

That event was five years ago. The path I have followed since has been one of the greatest journeys I have ever undertaken. In changing my perception of the world, my life has been transformed and I have been witness to so many beautiful and miraculous events.

The purpose of writing this book is to lead you into a new way of seeing and thinking. The ideas I present are fairly typical spiritual concepts, and I have set out my own personal experiences in this framework. Please realise that I am not trying to convert you to my way of thinking. At the end of the day, we can only make sense of the world through our own lens, based on our own experiences. All I am trying to demonstrate is that there is more than one way to view reality. The beliefs as set out in this book are based on my interpretation of reality. It doesn't mean to say it is right or accurate. But if it gives you peace, joy and happiness, and it helps make you a better person in the process, then who has the right to knock it. My hope is that the book will give you the courage to interpret reality in a way that serves you.

Once we set our minds free, we are on the path to a greater awareness. And that greater awareness helps you discover who you really are. Believe me when I say, you are more magnificent and amazing than you could ever know. You have incredible power and strength within you, to be whoever and to do whatever. Everything that you have ever wanted and needed is there inside yourself. You will still have struggles and obstacles to overcome, but awareness of spiritual principles and universal laws will give you the tools to tackle them in a much more effective way.

I have opened the book with a detailed account of my spiritual awakening; an event that is more common than people think. I have also included spiritual events that have happened to other members of my family that were life-changing for them. It also highlights that my experience is by no means unique. In our family alone, there are a few "spiritual stories" that abound. How many other families out there have similar stories that are buried or dismissed, for fear of being seen as crazy? Yet only by telling these stories, can we find the truth of who we are, and why we are here.

There may be ideas and concepts in the book that you find difficult to reconcile yourself with. That is fine. Just miss them out. It is set out in such a way that is not necessary to read everything. You can just pick the chapters that interest you. You may find some of the ideas "Too way out there." That is fine also. When I first started reading spiritual books, there were some ideas and thinking that I just couldn't even consider. They seemed too crazy. Yet when I was further along my path, and I went back to them a year later, they made perfect sense. My experience has taught me that the further you venture down the path, the more your mind, thoughts and ideas start to change. But it has to be a gradual process. It doesn't happen overnight. It is all part of the growth and awakening process.

Whilst I write this, the world seems a bit crazy right now and mental health is at an all time low. We have all these gadgets and possessions, but happiness is elusive, because we are looking in the wrong places. Our society teaches us that happiness is in all those things outside ourselves; the ideal partner, the better job, more money and material possessions. But this is a complete lie. To find true and deep happiness, we need to take the journey within. We need to heal our wounds and remove our blocks to happiness. And we need to operate from a place of love, rather than from a place of fear.

It takes great courage to shift your mind and thoughts, but I really hope that after reading this book, you will find the courage and determination within yourself to change your life and make it better than you could ever have dreamed possible. Believe me when I say that there really is a pot of gold. But it is not at the end of the rainbow. It is much closer than that. It lies within your very core. And you were meant to find it. It is your birthright and your entitlement. And when you do, you will truly understand that heaven is not a place. It is a state of mind. Good luck with your journey.

CHAPTER 1   MY AWAKENING

When you change the way you look at things,
The things you look at change.

Wayne Dyer

The truth of the matter is that I have always being fascinated by things that I could not understand. Whereas most people are wary and fearful of the unknown, I loved it. When I was 14, most girls my age were reading "Jackie", but I would have my head buried in the monthly magazine, "The unexplained." It really stirred my interest and I didn't get why others my age weren't interested in it. Instinctively, I felt that there was far more to life than what we have been led to believe. And over the years, I certainly had experiences that did not appear to have a rational explanation. But my true spiritual awakening arose when I was 47, following the death of my horse, Tiffany. The events that surrounded her death had a massive impact on me. And I learned an important lesson. When you are at your lowest point and in a state of total heartbreak, the most beautiful and profound things can occur.

When I lost Tiffany, my heart and mind had started to open. A few months before her death, I had discovered "Animal communication" and felt this was an answer to my prayer, to help me "talk" with animals. I was reading everything I could on the subject, and some of these books were so beautiful that I could feel my heart and mind opening with every word I read. I was so in awe of the process, that at night whilst asleep, I could feel the effects working on me – It was like my brain was being rewired. It was a strange but beautiful time.

And then Tiffany died. I recorded the story immediately after it happened, as I wanted the details to be as accurate as possible and I didn't want to leave anything out. This is what I wrote:

The night before I lost Tiffany, I had a beautiful dream, the like of which I have not had before or since. On awakening, I tried desperately to hold on to it, but the details evaded me. My only memory was spending the night with my horse, but not in the physical sense. More, on a soul level, where we were completely united and knew each other inside out. The dream affected me so much, that I mentioned it to my husband, who is by no means spiritual. His reaction was typical. I was just mad. Thinking about it now, I always knew that Tiffany and I had an incredible connection. I think it was her way of saying goodbye. But she was also telling me that nothing could ever separate us; that our souls would always be together.

Still in a daze from the dream, I went downstairs to make breakfast, and turned the computer on. I discovered the next beautiful thing to happen that morning. An animal communication (my first), had been carried out on Tiffany and was sitting in the inbox of my computer. It was meant to have been done a few weeks earlier, but through some strange twist, it had disappeared off the communicators list, so had been delayed until now. Today was clearly the day I was supposed to receive it, and with the events that were to follow, it was destined to become a parting gift. I was blown away – it was a wonderful testimony to our bond and adventures over the years, and it was completely accurate.

Before I even ventured up the stable yard that morning, everything seemed surreal. I had no idea that in just a few hours, I would lose my soul mate with whom I had spent 26 years. Although it was heartbreaking to say goodbye to my wonderful horse, I did draw comfort from the fact that I was with her throughout. Tiffany knew what was happening – she gave a loud neigh to her horse friend in the next field, and then to me. She made it very clear that she wanted me to stay with her. While we were waiting for the vet to arrive, she would rest her head on my shoulder, interspersed with walking around in very small circles. When doing this, she would be whinnying the whole time. It struck me as strange at the time – this was not a distressed "please save me" whinny, but very much a greeting whinny. I remembered just before my Nan died, she talked of a little boy and girl at the bottom of her bed, whom no-one else could see. Was this the same thing? Had her mother come for her? There was no doubt in my mind, that I was saying goodbye. As the vet walked up the path towards us, Tiffany spiralled in circles all the way up the field and collapsed in the gateway. The vet reckoned it was neurological.

The rest of the day passed in a haze of misery, as I went home and gave vent to my grief. In between the tears, I prayed fervently that my horse would be happy, and if possible that I could be given a sign to this effect. I just needed to know that she was happy and safe.

How quickly my prayer was answered. The very next day, I was riding along a bridle path, with my daughter and her friend, when we spotted a sunflower along the sandy path. I commented that I had never seen a sunflower on a bridleway before, and not one like this – it had a large head, but the stalk was short for a sunflower, being only about a foot off the ground. Even more remarkable, it was absolutely perfect. The petals were evenly spaced and it was without mark or flaw. The next day we rode past it again, but from the other direction. It looked even more surreal, this stunning sunflower next to the sandy path. It is the only time that I regretted having a £7 phone with no camera mode. The thought entered my head that it must be artificial, but as we rode past, there was no mistaking the leaves around its base and the thick stem entering the ground.

An hour later, when we rode back, the sunflower had gone. As my daughter expressed her astonishment, my numb, dazed brain clicked into gear and the full significance of what we had seen hit me. This was 9th March, not late summer, when you would expect to see a sunflower. And temperatures had plummeted to -5c the previous week. Furthermore, this bridleway is used by walkers and riders at the weekend, and yet the only ones to have witnessed it, were myself, my daughter and her friend. There was no doubt in my mind that this was the sign I had been so desperate to receive. And what a sign! For me, the sunflower radiates joy and happiness. Nothing could be better proof that my horse was residing in a beautiful place. I also felt instinctively, that she wanted me to experience the same joy and happiness. It wasn't just a symbol for her state of happiness, but also what she wanted for me.

16

Although I felt truly blessed and overjoyed to have received such a wondrous sign, and comforted to know my horse was happy, it was still hard to let go of the heartache inside. The thought of not seeing her on a daily basis, was hard to bear. Tuesday morning, I sat crying over my breakfast, wondering how I was going to face heading up the stables that morning. I was to put my friend's horses out, and their stables were right next to Tiffany's. How could I bear to hear them neigh to me, and for Tiff's neigh to be absent? On walking into the yard, my heart was very heavy. I was dreading the usual greeting. Instead, I could not believe what I was hearing, or rather not hearing. Just silence! I can honestly say that it is the only time in 8 years that they have not neighed to me, and the only time that I didn't want them to neigh.

Amazed, I stumbled into Esther's stable, to change her rug. The horse next to her, a beautiful thoroughbred named Monty, put his head over the wall. Normally, he is very aloof, and if I go to stroke him, he retreats. Today was different. He started nuzzling, kissing and licking me on the side of the neck. Loving this, I told him as much, and the more I praised him, the more intense it became. At one point, he put his head in front of mine and I had to look twice at what I was witnessing. His one eye had filled with water, and very slowly, a trickle ran down his face. To me, there was no doubt that this empathetic horse was picking up on my heartache. Not only this, but he was responding to it, and trying to comfort me. I recalled that he had lost his field mate only six months before – he understood the heartache of loss.

As I stood, mesmerised by what I was witnessing, Monty resumed kissing and licking the side of my neck. Up until now, Esther had been quietly standing by, but she suddenly became very interested in what Monty was doing. She looked at him quizzically, with a "what on earth are you doing" look on her face, and then unbelievably, she started to mimic what he was doing, on the other side of my neck. The next ten minutes passed in a blur. As these two horses gently caressed me, it felt like we were unified, in a bubble of harmony and love. Words can't do justice to the sense of empathy and understanding that the three of us were locked into. In all my years of being around horses, I have never had one horse, let alone two, lick my neck so lovingly. And these weren't even my horses. It was only when someone walked into the yard, and shouted "hello", that the spell was broken, and we all jumped apart.

Looking back, I realise something miraculous happened in that stable. The horses didn't just comfort me. They healed me and mended my heart in such a profound way, that even today, a few years on, I can't even comprehend it. I had walked into that stable with my heart breaking, and I walked out with a heart full of joy. I felt incredible happiness, like I had been touched by the divine. And through those horses, I believe that I had. My perception of my horse's death had changed completely, and I couldn't believe how much I had to be thankful for. It is very hard to explain, because it is something that I don't really understand, but from that moment I completely came to terms with my horse's death and felt only joy instead of heartache.

Needless to say, these events have changed my life. I have really opened up to the spiritual aspect of life and my perception of life (and death) has changed completely. From these experiences, I believe that death is only the body dying. I believe that the soul lives on, and our loved ones are always close to us, even though we can't see them. Separation is just an illusion! I also believe that by opening our hearts and minds, we can allow those souls to communicate with us, be it through dreams, meditation or other means. And I strongly believe that they want the same peace and happiness for us, as they themselves are experiencing. This is the message I get through all my communications. All they want is for us to experience joy, love and peace.

I realise that I was incredibly blessed to have had so much support, at such a difficult time, but I do believe that this is available to each and every one of us, if we allow it. I am no more special than the next person. All I did was open my heart and mind, and allow the impossible to happen. When we are prepared to take a leap of faith, and suppress our logical mind, the magic really does begin!

I wrote the above, to preserve its accuracy. Over the years, I have passed it on to friends who have lost animals, and they tell me that it has brought them a great deal of comfort. I feel so happy, that it has helped other people and given them strength, at those times when they really needed it.

I have come to appreciate more and more, the significance of the sunflower. It speaks to me on so many levels. As well as communicating to me that my horse was residing in a joyous place, my research on the symbolic meaning of the sunflower has unearthed some hugely relevant facts. It has very strong spiritual connotations. In Christianity, the sunflower is a symbol of God's love. God had clearly demonstrated his love to me in answering my heartfelt prayer. Another spiritual interpretation relates to the way that the sunflower seeks and turns its head towards the sun, seeking out the light. In this respect, is it not encouraging our soul to do the very same thing? Certainly for me, there is no denying that the sunflower I witnessed was pivotal in my spiritual journey; leading me down a path that was so much lighter and brighter than anything I had known before. Like the sunflower, I am now a seeker of light.

I now want to tell other stories that have been passed down from family members, and which are no less miraculous. In every case, these events were life-changing, and impressed upon the recipient a different version of reality. In all the stories there is a degree of suffering involved; in the case of my Nan, it was physical suffering – she was literally dying; in my dad's case, it was extreme emotional suffering – fearing for the health of my mum and his unborn child (me); in the case of my great-aunt it was despair at losing her parents and being the sole-breadwinner; and in the case of my granddad, it was mental suffering.

My Nan's story (my mother's mum)

My Nan's story is truly miraculous. There is no other word for it. She told me this story on a number of occasions, and the details never changed. I loved hearing it, and seeing my Nan light up as she was telling it. She was a stickler for telling the truth and recounting tales exactly as they occurred. In fact my Nan was very quiet, and I actually wonder how many people she told this story to. My Dad mentioned recently that she had never recounted it to him. He heard the story from my mum.

As a child, my Nan had been very ill and had been unable to attend school. She had to use a wheelchair, but the doctors didn't know what was wrong. They just said that she would never be able to work, marry, or have children, and she would probably die before she became an adult. When she was 12, she was very ill in bed and everyone thought she was dying. A man came to the door asking for water. My Great-grandmother apologised, saying that she couldn't let him in because her child was dying. She closed the door and went to attend to my Nan. To her amazement, my Nan was sitting up in bed, begging her to please find that man who had healed her. Although my great-grandmother ran up and down the road, there was no sign of him, and none of the other neighbours had seen him. From that day, my Nan went on to make a full recovery, without the wheelchair. By 14 she was working, and she went on to marry and have three children. She lived until she was 94 years old, and at 90, her doctor on giving her a full health check, remarked he had never come across a healthier person of that age. There is absolutely no doubt in my mind that my Nan had been healed by an angel and this was her belief also.

On reflection, my Nan in a lot of ways was other worldly. She was not religious or spiritual, but she embodied the qualities of a Godly person. She was incredibly humble, and probably the most selfless person I have ever come across. Completely disinterested in material possessions, she would have given her last penny away. The only thing I ever remember my Nan coveting, were her books. She loved reading, and would devour a book in a couple of days. As she never had the opportunity to attend school, it was my granddad who taught her to read and write, and she clearly cherished and revelled in this gift until she died.

Dad's story

My mum was four months pregnant with me, and throughout the pregnancy she had been terribly sick. This particular day had been worse than normal. The sickness had been continuous all day. Mum went to bed at 6pm, exhausted. Dad put a bucket by the side of the bed, which was used regularly over the next few hours. Dad always said his prayers by the bed, and this particular night at about 10pm, he knelt down as usual. To say that my dad was scared was an understatement. He was absolutely terrified – both for my mum's wellbeing and for my own. Fear was really taking hold as he worried about losing either my mum or me. His prayers that night were a plea for help. He just let down his defences and prayed from the heart. Immediately he got a message. Dad admits that how he got the message is a bit odd to explain. He said it was like someone had spoken to him from a few feet away, and he was remembering it. And the message was very clear. "Don't worry, she will be fine. There is a reason for her being this sick. But she won't be as sick again. From today she will start to get better."Ten minutes later when my Dad got up from his prayers, my mum was asleep. And from that day as promised, she was much better and only sick on the odd occasion. My Dad has never doubted for a single second that they were words spoken by God in response to his prayer.

My Great- Aunt's story (on dad's side)

My granddad was 15 when his dad died. Two years later, his mother, it is said, died of a broken-heart. His oldest sister was 21, and as well as my granddad, there were another two sisters to take care of. Laura, the eldest, was a secretary. And now with their parents dead, she was also head of the household. She was struggling to cope, and finding the responsibility of caring for three younger siblings, a huge weight on her shoulders. One day she took a bus ride to Sedgley. She needed a walk in the countryside to get her head together, and to take time out for herself. As she was walking, she heard a very clear voice that said "Laura". The voice was not in her head. It was outside herself, and she instantly recognised it as her mother's. She looked around, but there was nobody in sight. The voice continued, "Laura, pull yourself together for the sake of the family." To hear her mother telling her this, was everything she needed to hear. She took her mum's advice, and pulled herself together. For the rest of her life, she never doubted for a single second that her mother had spoken to her.

Grandad's story (Dad's dad)

My grandad's story isn't as dramatic as the others, and to some, it may appear quite trivial, but I am including it, because it made a huge impression on him.

My granddad was very involved with the church. When war broke out, he was really bothered by the fact that the first building to be bombed in England was a church. In fact, it bothered him that much, that he actually had a few sleepless nights over it. A few nights of this, and he suddenly heard a voice say, "Arthur, do you really think I would protect my buildings from bombing, when other buildings are being destroyed?" My granddad was so happy to hear this that he never worried about it again. For the rest of his life, he was convinced that God had spoken directly to him.

Unfortunately my Grandad died when I was only five years old, but I still recall a man who was incredibly gentle and loving. My mum describes him as a saint. I like to think that hearing the voice of God really buoyed his faith, shaping him into the beautiful person he was.

In all these experiences, none of the recipient's doubted the divinity behind them for a single second. They were also all happy to tell others what had happened. This is particularly unusual for the older generations, because they lived in an age where such things were very much hushed up. Hearing voices was seen as the first sign of madness. In my case, I was happy to tell the whole world. Why keep something so wonderful to yourself? As well as friends and family, everyone on the yard became familiar with the story, as did the butchers and bakers (but not the candlestick makers). I just wanted people to know that there is more to life than what we are brought up to believe. After all, if a flower can just appear and then disappear again, then what does this say about physical laws? They are not as real as we think, and there is a lot more going on than we care to admit.

 Over the years, I have heard the most amazing and beautiful stories from people. I have not included them here, as they are not my stories to tell, but I do encourage everyone to speak up. Only by talking about spiritual matters can we truly come to terms with our divinity and the fact that there is far more to life than we realise. By discovering the truth, life will be so much easier for all of us. It is time the veil of illusion was lifted.

CHAPTER 2   LIFE'S PURPOSE

You are not a drop in the ocean
You are the entire ocean in a drop.

Rumi

For as long as I remember, I have always believed that our life has purpose and meaning. When I look around me, I see a world that is so incredibly intricate, beautiful and intelligent. By its very design, there has to be a higher intelligence behind its existence. There is no way that creation was just an accident! I refer to this higher intelligence as "God", or "the universe", but really it can be called whatever you want to refer to it. Through the events in my life, and the multitude of stories that people have confided in me, I have absolutely no doubt whatsoever that there is a higher intelligence at work. But I don't think of God as a person. More, a loving, intelligent essence, and I also believe that each one of us contains this divine essence. In this sense, we are all connected. Not just with each other, but with animals and nature. We are all part of a divine wholeness and oneness. Now that I am much further along my spiritual path, I am really starting to get this concept. It is getting easier to see the divine light in other people. Even when people are in negative mode, and they are moaning and complaining about everyone and everything, I can still see the beauty and the good in them.

It is my belief that we are essentially spirits, and have chosen to come to earth in a body and have a physical experience. Our earthly life subjects us to the highs and lows of life as a human being. We experience a whole range of emotions, from love, hate, joy and despair. By experiencing all this, we learn to evolve and grow. There are so many lessons to learn in the school of life! We have many incarnations, and through each one, there are different lessons to learn. In one life we may be poor, and struggle to survive, but in another life we may be rich. Every situation we find ourselves in and the difficulties we face are all opportunities for growth.

Reincarnation

Most spiritual thinking is centred round the idea that we keep reincarnating so that we can evolve; the aim being to attain enlightenment. When we reach enlightenment, we no longer have to return to the physical realm, as we have learned all the lessons that are necessary. We can remain in heaven.

There is so much evidence for reincarnation. Ian Stevenson has been a pioneer for research and investigation into reincarnation, and his evidence for it is very compelling. He studied no less than 3000 child cases of reincarnation, and published his work in various books on the subject. His work makes for fascinating reading. He discovered that birthmarks and defects, could relate to past life injuries. Also, many children had unusual abilities, or phobias, which could not be attributed to their current life. But more compelling, some children were able to give very specific details about where they had lived in past lives, as well as providing detailed information of their families and how they had lived and died. And investigations into their claims showed that they matched up. There was one fascinating case which was reported in the newspapers, of a boy who not only identified the location of his murdered body, but also the man who murdered him. Faced with this accusation, the murderer, who was still alive, actually confessed to his crime.

I have always been intrigued by reincarnation, due to my own childhood experiences. As a very young child, I always felt I was a boy, and couldn't understand why people would refer to me as a girl. Also, I was very wary and scared of people, even though I was born into an extremely loving family. As a baby, I would scream at people who tried to talk to me, but I adored animals. My parents found that if they lay me in a certain position in the lounge, I would cry. When I was older, I told them it was because I could see a witches face in the woodwork surrounding the fire. But what does a baby know about witches? Also, when I was about three years old I used to have recurring dreams, where spirits would appear. But what does a child so young know about spirits? There seems to have been so much fear in my early years, but unless you could relate these to a past life, I don't know where else these fears originated from. There was certainly nothing in my current life, that could account for them, as I had no negative experiences whatsoever in those early years.

Path of the soul

It is widely believed in spiritual circles that the soul makes a contract before it comes to the earthly plain, setting out the lessons it needs to evolve, and around this, the major events in its life, including the parents it is born to, the place it is born and the time of its death. When death does occur, a review of the soul's life is undertaken, to clarify the lessons learned, but this is in no way judgemental.

The very first spiritual course I attended, people were telling me that we choose our parents. I couldn't get this at all. Yes, I adore my parents and would pick them every time, but not everyone is this lucky. For instance, why would you pick parents that abuse and hurt you? As with all questions in life, we tend to approach them with our human mind. In time, you learn to view these sort of questions from a much wider perspective, although it has taken time for me to be able to do this. I now realise that there are all sorts of reasons why you may choose to pick less than ideal parents. It may be to accelerate your growth, and learn lessons such as forgiveness; it may be to teach your parents about responsibility and love – some people do change when they have children; or it may be to highlight social issues and bring about changes in law. We don't necessarily come to earth to work on our own growth. We may also choose to work on other peoples, recognising that we are all connected.

Soul purpose

In the spiritual world, there is a lot of emphasis on finding your "true purpose" and how you can serve the world. Some argue that the best way you can serve the world, is by being authentic and living a joyful, loving life. This makes a lot of sense to me. If you are a loving and joyful person, this impacts hugely on the people around you. Your positive energy helps to release positivity and a chain reaction is set off.

I think that every person on earth at some point has questioned, "Why are we here and what is it all for?" Most people feel at some point in their lives a sense that they should be doing something, or the feeling of emptiness. That is why people who seem to have everything in life – career, success, money, beautiful family, good health – can still be unhappy or depressed. Outwardly they have achieved everything, but inwardly they have achieved nothing and they know on a soul level, that something is missing.

The journey to find out about your soul requires a deep level of willingness, courage and determination. You need to set aside previous beliefs and understandings, and this can take tremendous courage.

Before I set out on my spiritual path, some nights I would have very frightening dreams. On awakening, I would be really shaken, but they would always leave me with an acute sense of good and evil in the world, and the battle between the two. I would be saying to myself, "I want to be on the side of good." Once I stepped on to my spiritual path, they stopped. I do believe that the dreams were my soul's reminder that I had come here to do something positive and to make a difference in the world; to create more light and extinguish the darkness. Yes, it might only be a bit part, but if all of us listened to our soul's call, we could change the world.

If you are interested in finding out what your soul's agenda is, then the clues are in the things that bring you enjoyment. What makes you tick? What brings you great happiness? Our passions in life are a clue as to why we are here. When we are doing the things we love, then our hearts dance and our souls sing. This energises us, and raises our vibration. We become the best version of ourselves, and as a result, we are more in touch with our divine selves. This not only increases our own happiness – but it affects all the people around us too. They feel lighter and happier, for having this positive energy around them. Everyone's a winner!

I don't think our brains are sophisticated enough to comprehend the complete truth of our existence. We can only gain as much knowledge as our brains allow. When we die, I believe that everything will become clear and the truth will out. So, why do we lose our knowledge when we are born and why do we lose sight of our life's purpose? I think we have to forget everything that has come before. If we were aware of our previous lives, and we knew the answers, I don't think we could really learn our lessons. It would be too easy. We are introduced to a wide range of emotions in our earthly life, and these are essential for our growth, and to teach us compassion and empathy.

I do believe that each and every one of us has a part to play in the workings of the world. We are all part of the tapestry of life. This is hard for most people to accept. There are so many people alive in the world, at any one moment, that it seems that we are like the grains of sand in a desert. As an individual, we believe we can't possibly make an impact on the world. But on the contrary, one of the common features of the Near Death experience is the understanding that not only do our actions and words matter, but even our thoughts affect the Universe. We are changing things in the Universe, just by what we are thinking, as it is those thoughts that lead to actions. This is a bit like the butterfly effect – it has been claimed that a butterfly flapping its wings in New Mexico, can cause a hurricane in China.

Actions have consequences

Our actions can have a massive effect on others. Everything that we do has a consequence. I don't think we realise how far-reaching those consequences can be and how many people can be affected by a single action. Again, this just goes to show how connected we really are to each other.

Theresa Cheung talks about this in her book, "The ten signs of heaven". She tells the story of her mother, who was greatly affected by her near death experience. To her surprise, in the heavenly realms, she wasn't met by any family members, but by a woman she didn't recognise. This woman reminded her of her huge kindness. They had been queuing for cinema tickets, and before the woman could acquire one, they were sold out. Theresa's mother saw the distress on this young woman's face, and so passed over her own ticket, as she could see that it meant more to this woman than it did to her. As the young woman made her way to her seat, she knocked over a cornet of popcorn. She apologised to the young man, and they started a conversation. This led to them dating and eventually marrying, and they had two children. A few years later, she was killed in a car crash. The reason she felt so much gratitude to Theresa's mum, was because those few years she was with that man were the happiest of her life. For the first time, she understood the meaning of true love. It was an act of kindness that Theresa's mother did not think twice about, but it was an act that completely changed someone else's life.

I love this story. It demonstrates how our actions, even though seemingly insignificant and inconsequential at the time, can actually have a massive and far-reaching effect on other people's lives. This also shows we are more connected to each other than we think.

Connectedness

In our society, we are brought up with the idea that we are not only separate from each other, but we are also separate from nature and everything else in the Universe. Competition exacerbates separation. From a very early age, competition is encouraged and is seen as a good thing in our society. Through competition, we can strive to be better than everyone else, and get the best jobs and make more money etc. But all this does, is separate us from our fellow man. It also creates a lot of negative emotions, such as ruthlessness and jealousy. We are constantly comparing ourselves with others, and that feeling that we are not good enough becomes pervasive.

I believe in the idea that we are all connected – not just with each other, but with everything in the Universe. We are part of the great whole. In this respect, the Universe exists inside us. Those people who are truly enlightened recognise that sense of oneness with all things; not just other people, but with animals, nature, and the very earth herself. They recognise we are all part of the same whole.

If only more people believed in this concept – we could get rid of inequality, racial tension, terrorism and wars. Humans would come to realise that when they hurt other people, or even their environment, by the same token, they are hurting themselves. I learned this lesson, when I was very young. I fell out with a friend, and swung my pump bag at her, causing her a black eye. She wasn't allowed out of the house for a week, because her parents were so embarrassed by her appearance, and probably worried that they may be seen as the perpetrators. I can still recall the terrible guilt and shame I felt. I didn't like myself at all, and promised myself that I would never strike out at anyone again, even in self defence. It wasn't worth losing my peace of mind for. This was a huge lesson for me.

The near death experience (NDE)

The NDE can teach us an awful lot about why we are here. More and more people are experiencing this, probably because it is now much easier to resuscitate people and bring them back from the dead. And the accounts of NDE's can teach us an awful lot about our purpose for being here. Since a teenager, I have read hundreds of accounts recounted by people who have had an NDE, and I have always been struck by the similarities in the stories. And this is the thing; if the brain was still able to function for a while after being clinically dead, people may experience things, but surely the accounts would all be very different. Instead, they are very similar, irrespective of race, beliefs and religion. Most stories feature one or more of the following:-

- Consciousness leaving the body. People see themselves outside their body. They can see the people around them, hear the conversations going on, and what is being done to try and resuscitate them. There are also accounts of instant teleportation to somewhere else on the physical plane. For example, people have reported seeing their relatives boarding planes thousands of miles away, and being aware of their conversations. There are some amazing accounts, which have convinced doctors and nurses of the validity of the claim.

- Venturing down a tunnel of light. Again, this is very common.

- Encountering angels and departed loved ones.

- Being witness to your whole life's journey. In seconds or minutes, you see a flashback of your whole life.

- Having a life review. You see parts of your life, where you acted lovingly and nobly, and parts of your life, where you didn't act so graciously. There is no judgement passed; it just seems that you are shown these things to become clearer as to how you should have acted.

- Being told that it is not your time to pass to heaven; you still have much to do on earth and you need to go back.

- Being given the answers to everything. This seems to be downloaded in seconds.

- Communicating with everyone through telepathy.

- Being aware of incredible love, joy and peace.

- Realising that space and time is an illusion.

- For those who remain longer in heaven, being aware of beautiful buildings and surroundings. Noting that the colours are more vivid and wider ranging, and having a sense of it being more real than the physical reality on earth.

There will always be sceptics and people who choose not to believe these accounts. But one of the most convincing aspects of the NDE, is the lives these people lead when they come back to the physical plane. Relatives and friends find them much changed from before. They seem to bring back the lessons they learned in the afterlife. They understand the oneness of life and our connection with each other and the universe; they understand the importance of love; their lives are lived with much more purpose and joy; they lose the ability to feel fear; death no longer worries them. And a lot of them take the spiritual path, devoting their life to writing and talking to the rest of us, trying to convince us that there is nothing to fear.

Alexander Eben is one such person. He was a highly successful American neurosurgeon, who had graduated from Harvard. He never believed in an afterlife, and although a lot of his patients discussed NDE's with him, he dismissed them as effects of the drugs. That is until he had his own NDE. He developed bacterial meningitis, and was in a coma for seven days. During that time his brain was completely dead, and as a neurosurgeon he knew that it was not possible to experience anything. Yet he not only journeyed to the afterlife; his experience, he described later was more real than life on earth. In addition, he met his sister, even though he had never even been aware of her existence. It was only later, when he returned to the physical plane that it was revealed to him that he had a sister, who had died when she was young, and on seeing her photograph, he recognised her as the girl who had accompanied him in the afterlife. Since coming back to the physical realm, Dr Eben has devoted his life to spirituality. He has written two books about his NDE and travels around the world giving talks on the subject.

Scientific Opinion

Theresa Cheung is a great author, who has written a lot of books dedicated to proving heaven is real. Her books are based on the thousands of accounts that people have sent to her over the years. She is particularly interested in closing the gap between science and spirituality, and with this in mind, she interviews leading scientists, doctors and researchers. It would seem from the interviews she has carried out, that scientists are starting to come around to the idea that consciousness can exist outside the body. Leading the way is resuscitation expert Dr Sam Parnia, an assistant professor at the State University of New York, and a former research fellow at the University of Southampton. Parnia believes his work proves that consciousness can exist outside the body and survive brain death. His groundbreaking 2014 NDE study got all the major newspapers talking, and his research is so convincing that scientists have had no choice but to sit up and take notice.

Modern quantum research and theory is also forwarding the idea that there may be life after death. Influential supporters from the medical and scientific community, such as Deepak Chopra, Dean Radin and Robert Lanza, base their beliefs on the idea that the universe is a product of our consciousness, and not the other way around, as some scientists would have us believe. In other words, time, space, matter, life, death and everything else only exist because of our perception of them.

Then there is the idea put forward by some quantum scientists of a parallel universe, where we are living parallel lives. At this moment in time, this is a bit more than my brain is able to contemplate.

A few years ago, the editor of the New Scientist magazine posed the question, "What is reality?" Various writers, presumably scientists, suggested answers, but it transpired that each suggested solution had at least one flaw. The conclusion they arrived at, was that whatever reality is, it isn't what it seems. That is, it isn't what scientists think it might be. In truth, there probably isn't a person alive who knows all the answers. We will have to wait until death to learn the truth.
`

In the meantime, all we can do is to live a meaningful life. If our life has purpose, which I very much believe it does, then each one of us has come to earth to fulfil a role. To do this, it is important that we discover and act in accordance with our true selves. This is explored in more detail in the next chapter.

CHAPTER 3   BE TRUE TO YOURSELF

Dip into your own soul
Find your own truth
What calls to your heart
What moves your spirit.
Make your life dance
To the song of your own essence

Cherokee Billie

I believe that at our core, we are all beings of love. We are all born with that divine essence inside us. In spiritual circles, this divine essence is known as "our higher self." As children, we are very much tuned into our higher selves, but as we grow we become more disconnected from our higher selves. We start to lose sight of who we really are. In our quest to fit in and be accepted, we start to act and take on roles that we think are expected of us. We try to become the people that others want us to be. Some people model themselves on someone they admire – seeking to dress the same, look the same, and think the same. They lose themselves in their quest to become someone else. In doing so, they imprison themselves and bury their soul.

All of us at some point in our lives feel that we are different to everyone else. That sense of not belonging; of being different, is very common. We feel lonely and misunderstood, and wish we could be "normal" like everyone else. The reason we feel this way is because we are different to everyone else. Each one of us is completely unique. No one else sounds likes us, looks like us or thinks like us. Each one of us has our own special talents and gifts to bring forth into the world. There is not a single person alive who is not gifted at something. When you say this to people, they immediately pipe up with "I haven't found my gift yet." But gifts don't just refer to being clever, artistic, musical or sporty. The meaning is much wider. Some people are brilliant carers, or homemakers, and others are brilliant at making people laugh or helping others feel good about themselves. Believe me when I say "You have a beautiful gift. Cherish it, be grateful for it, and make the most of it. Use it for the benefit of others, for when you do, you will start to learn the meaning of true happiness."

Imprisoned by society

It is such a shame that we live in a society that does not celebrate people's uniqueness and individuality. Instead, our society tries to crush our individuality, leaving us in a desperate bid to be "normal", to "fit in," to be like everyone else. Well, let me put you straight. There is no normal. It does not exist. There is no such thing. What is normal to one person is completely abnormal to another. It is a completely pointless exercise. We are all created as unique beings, with different gifts and talents, to bring balance to the world. Most people respond well to a good talker; someone who cheers you up and knows how to say the right thing. But equally, a good talker needs a good listener. They are both just as important, and the one can't exist without the other. Everyone needs to be valued in their own right.

It makes me very sad that our society treats people with disabilities or people that are impaired in some way, as not being normal. These people may have a different way of viewing the world, but who is to say that their perception of the world is in any way less correct than the way other people perceive reality. This realisation came to me one day, when I was shopping in the village.

I had wandered into the bakery, and there was a young Down's syndrome man in his twenties, talking to the shop assistants. It transpired that they knew him, and hadn't seen him for some time, as he had moved out of the village. I am very good at reading people's energy, and this young man had the most beautiful energy. I was fascinated with him. One of the women asked him if he was happy, and he enthused that he was extremely happy and really enjoying life. He radiated joy and happiness. I walked into the butchers, and he followed me in. He made a big fuss of all the people serving. He could remember all their names, but not one could remember his. The greeting he gave them all was so warm, genuine and joyful. Again, I bathed in his beautiful, joyful and loving energy. Witnessing the way he conducted himself, really made me question our version of normality. Here was this man, welcoming people so joyfully and lovingly, with no embarrassment or self consciousness. He was acting from his true core, with no attempt to be something that he wasn't. It really makes you question – who is the most normal? In my opinion, it was him. I can only aspire to be like this man.

From the moment you are born into this world, you are subject to a form of brainwashing; from your parents, your teachers, your friends, but mostly from society. Western society, with its emphasis on materialism and outer beauty, has a lot to answer for, and shapes your behaviour and way of thinking. And there is only one reason for this. Greed! Individuals and companies are making huge profits from our materialistic desires. We are shaped and modelled from a very young age, to be the ideal consumer. One such example is the beauty industry. By promoting young people's vanity, they can ensure that beauty products and cosmetic procedures are in massive demand, and this brings in huge profits. But these profits are made at a price. And the price is the mental health of our young people. If only our society put more emphasis on inner beauty. If only young people could be taught how to tap into wisdom and how to love and value themselves.

The same can be said for our use of medicines. For every illness or discomfort, there is a pill to pop, or a cream to apply. Pharmaceutical companies have made a fortune from our health issues. But here is an interesting fact. One indigenous Tribe I was reading about are not allowed to use medicines. They believe that all illnesses have a pseudo-spiritual dimension to it. For every ailment, they will only use a cactus tree. And here is the surprising thing. They live long and healthy lives. In fact, when they reach the grand old age of 100, they partake in a 500km pilgrimage, completing it quicker than Westerners a third of their age.

There is no denying the fact that if you had been born into another society, your beliefs and thoughts would be radically different. If you had been born as a shaman or born into an indigenous tribe, you would have very different values and thinking. Your life would be lived in a way that honoured the earth and you would practise a deep reverence for nature. The idea of self would disappear, and community based living would be all important. You would also be very aware of the invisible realms and working with spirits would be normal. This just goes to show how much society shapes your thinking. You are a servant to your society.

Both men and women are victims of the restrictions that society imposes on us. Women from certain cultures are still regarded as subservient to men, and with this thinking in force, they have no voice whatsoever. I appreciate that for these women, it is very difficult to be their true selves. If this is the situation you find yourself in, please do not give up hope. Know that in God's eyes we are all equal. Please be patient. If humanity is to evolve and move forward, then there must be change.

It isn't just women who are affected. Men are too, although not so clearly. For men, showing emotion is still very much seen as a weakness. Young boys are commonly told to "man up" or to "stop being a girl's blouse." Statements like this are very damaging. Expressing emotion is very healthy and should be encouraged. Suppressing emotions can lead to depression and illness. Crying is a great release, and is far healthier than trying to bury the feeling. Suicide amongst men is far higher than amongst women, and I do believe that it is this suppression of emotion that is the trigger.

My personal story

From a young age, I felt very connected to nature and animals. I loved nothing better than being out in the countryside. For me, being in nature was incredibly healing and restorative. From the age of 12, I became involved with horses, and for me this was a lifeline. As I grew, I became increasingly uncomfortable in a world that to me, didn't make any sense; a world that values logical thinking over everything and which is drowned in material possessions, and obsessed with outer beauty. As a sensitive child, I couldn't understand why there was so much violence and hatred. I was living in a world that I just couldn't relate to. Added to this, I was very shy and introverted. Yet this was a world that expected women to talk, talk, talk. But, I was one of the lucky ones. I was surrounded by family and friends who loved me for who I was. And when I was with horses, I lived in a world that did make sense. Around the horses, there was no need to talk. I could converse with them in other ways. Escaping into the countryside while astride a horse was complete heaven for me. I was so very lucky to have had this in my life.

Through my spiritual journey, I have now discovered my true self, and all the jigsaw pieces fit into place. I had never even heard of a shaman until a couple of years ago, but I now realise that I am far more a shaman, than I am a westerner. Shamans recognise that everything has life force energy and intelligence. They honour earth, animals, trees and plants, and recognise the connection we have with all of nature. They interact with the invisible realms, harnessing the power of spirit guides and power animals. They also recognise the wisdom that is contained in dreams. I have always been a dreamer, and as a child, had a very creative imagination. This and my deep connection to nature, has made me think I was born into the wrong society. I mentioned this recently to a friend, and very wisely she stated "There are no mistakes. You may have a shaman head, but you were born into this society to open this way of thinking to the rest of us." Yes, she is right! And she has made a good point. We are all here to teach each other, and to appreciate everyone's different perspective on life.

Breaking free

We are so afraid to be ourselves; but why? What is the worst that could happen? Are we afraid of being laughed at, or worse, rejected? But do we really want friends around us that would treat us this way? Surely it is much better to be accepted for whom we are, than who we are trying to be. Now that I am older and wiser, I have no qualms about being my true self. If people want to see me as crazy, then fine. Let them. By being my true self, I attract like-minded people, who I can relate to and enjoy being with. I would much rather be around people who appreciate me for who I am.

When you stop worrying about what other people think about you, it is akin to breaking free from prison. It is wonderful to be your true self, talking about the things that really resonate with you, and not worrying about how others will react. After all, they can always wander off and find someone else to talk to, if it doesn't interest them. But by the same token, you will always attract someone like-minded, who finds your conversation interesting and wants to join in.

We can spend so much time trying to please other people or conform to social norms, that we can lose sight of our own identity and who we truly are. This can lead to us becoming so disconnected from our authentic selves that we become unhappy and depressed. This doesn't mean that we have to become selfish, and get our own way in everything. It just means that we need to consider our own needs.

In her book "Dying to be me", Anita Moorjani, writes about her Near Death experience. She claims that one of the most important things she learned was to be authentic. She realised that she had spent all her life trying to please others and live up to their expectations. In the process, she had neglected herself and her own needs. The valuable lesson she learned, was that you need to take care of yourself first. For when you are in a happy and balanced state, then you are in a much better position to help others.

I am finishing this chapter with a quote and poem from Anita, which I believe holds a great deal of wisdom. If we all lived by this, we would be much happier.

"If you are true to yourself, you will enjoy your life and attract into your life what is truly yours. If you

listen to your heart, and do things with your heart, you can't go wrong. The universe will oblige and help you. It really is that simple. The more you try to be someone you're not, the more you push away what you deserve. The reason we deny our truth is fear – fear of not being good enough or pretty enough or clever enough or deserving enough. Just believe that you are enough and be yourself with joy and without fear and then you will attract what is truly yours."

"When I was born into this world
The only things I knew were to love, laugh and shine my light brightly.
Then as I grew people told me to stop laughing.
"Take life seriously" they said,
"If you want to get ahead in this world."
So I stopped laughing.
People told me, "Be careful who you love
If you don't want your heart broken."
So I stopped loving.
They said, "Don't shine your light so bright
As it draws too much attention onto you."
So I stopped shining.
And became small
And withered
And died
Only to learn upon death
That all that matters in life
Is to love, laugh and shine our light brightly!"

CHAPTER 4   THE EGO (THE ENEMY WITHIN)

If you want to reach a state of bliss, then go beyond your ego and the internal dialogue. Make a decision to relinquish the need to control, the need to be approved, and the need to judge.

Deepak Chopra

One of the surprising absences in spiritual books is reference to the Devil. None of the books ever seem to mention him. But surely, if there is a God, representative of all the good in the world, then there must be a Devil, responsible for all the evil? After all, we need someone to blame for our shortcomings and for the dark side of our nature.

Most Spiritual thinking puts the blame for all the evil and wrong doing in the world squarely at the feet of us. It is our ego that is to blame for the bad in the world. The ego is seen as the enemy within, which needs taming and controlling. It is that voice in our head, which encourages us to be competitive, jealous, fearful, controlling, manipulative, judgemental; all those negative qualities that when taken to extreme, results in murder, wars and mayhem. The ego encourages us to believe that we are separate from everyone else and separate from God. It encourages cohesiveness and division. In simplistic terms, the ego represents our human mind, in all its limitation; that primitive part of our mind that believes in looking after oneself, forsaking all others. In this manner, it tries to keep us separate from our true self; our higher, divine consciousness. In short, the ego is a mind where God is absent.

It is very clear that fear and judgemental thinking create so many problems in the world today. We judge others because it makes us feel better about ourselves. Fear of different religions and races has resulted in conflict and wars, since man first walked the earth. Recently, the decision to leave the EU was based on people's fear of immigration. Political parties and the Media like to stir up this fear based thinking. It wins political campaigns, it sells newspapers. But at the end of the day, this fear and hatred mean we are all losers in the Game of life. Many people during their lifetime will be a victim of robbery, violence or assault. All results of a fear based and egotistic society.

Judgemental thinking

Judging others is one of the egos favourite pastimes. I consider myself far less judgemental now than previously, but even I have trouble going a whole day without passing judgement on someone or something. Try it, because it is not as easy as you think. As we grow from children to adults, passing judgement seems to become part of our nature.

The truth is that none of us have the right to judge. None of us can know the circumstances of a person's life, to bring them where they are today. This goes for past lives, as well as current life. Any of us in past lives may have committed murders, evil acts etc. But as our soul evolves, and we start to learn and grow from the lessons we are given, we become more loving and compassionate. In this respect, we are all equal and no one person is any better than another. It is just that some people have had more lifetimes to evolve than other people and so they are further along their path of evolutionary growth.

As a child, I was the victim of bullying at school. I was only seven years old, and witnessed a classmate being physically harassed by another girl. I went to her rescue. The effects were disastrous for me. The victim joined forces with the bully and another girl, and the three of them turned their hatred on me. Even now, nearly 50 years on, I still remember it like it was only yesterday. The fear that I felt before home time each evening was terrible. They would tie me to a lamppost and pummel me, and although I have no memory of the physical harm they bestowed on me, the emotional trauma was embedded in me for a long time. It was only when the two girls left school, as we transferred from Infant to Middle School that the bullying stopped.

The one thing that came out of this, and the one thing that I am proud of, is that I never judged or hated them. With the loving compassion that is natural to most children, I understood why they had acted that way. The victim had joined them to save her own skin. While they were picking on someone else, she was safe. It was self-preservation. Not the best action to take however, because the guilt probably preyed on her mind for a long time afterwards. I also felt this was the same reason why the other girl joined in. As for the ringleader, I just felt sorry for her. Before she picked on me, I went to her house the once, the way all children do, when they are young. I can still picture her mum, and let's just say that she was not like any other mum I had encountered before. I was left with the feeling that here was a girl that was neglected and unwanted; not loved and cherished like I was. I felt a lot of bitterness and hatred in her house; a very different feeling from the love and warmth in my own house, so I understood why she acted the way she did. Her treatment of others was probably a reflection of the treatment that was being meted out to her.

Recently, on the Internet, there was a really good story, portraying why we should never judge others. It is a brilliant example, of how we can never truly know the full facts behind a perceived story. What can appear as one thing, can be something completely different. A bit like a magician's trick, things aren't always as they seem. I have recreated it below because I think it is a great example of why we need to keep an open mind.

A teacher was addressing her class and started to tell them a story.

A cruise ship met with an accident at sea. On the ship was a couple, who after having made their way to the lifeboat, realised there was only one space left. At this moment, the man pushed the woman behind him and jumped into the lifeboat himself. The lady stood on the sinking ship and shouted one sentence to her husband.

The teacher stopped and asked "What do you think she shouted?" Most of the students excitedly answered, "I hate you, I was blind!"

Now the teacher noticed a boy who was silent throughout. She got him to answer and he replied, "Teacher, I believe she would have shouted, "Take care of our child!"

The teacher was surprised, asking "Have you heard this story before?" The boy shook his head. "Nope, but that was what my mum told my dad before she died to disease."

The teacher lamented, "The answer is right." The cruise sunk, the man went home and brought up their daughter single-handedly. Many years later, after the death of the man, their daughter found his diary while tidying his belongings. It turns out that when the parents went onto the cruise ship, the mother was already diagnosed with terminal illness. At the critical moment, the father rushed to the only chance of survival. He wrote in his diary, "How I wished to sink to the bottom of the ocean with you. But for the sake of our daughter, I can only let you live forever below the sea alone."

Ego's attempts to keep you small

A large and inflated ego conjures up a person who is big-headed and a know it all. But, the ego can conspire to deflate you, as much as inflate you. Thoughts such as "Am I clever enough, pretty enough, attractive enough, interesting, popular etc.", all stem from the ego trying to take control.

I regularly have an original insight pop into my head, that I know is divinely inspired, because someone else benefits. These ideas originate from my higher/true self. But the sad thing is, I rarely carry them through. My ego takes over, and I talk myself out of it. These insecurities are the ego's greatest weapon, and by wielding it, there can be no moving forward with your life. You are stuck! A typical battle between the ego and the true self is along the following lines:-

True self: Everyone keeps telling me I should write a spiritual book. So maybe I should.

Ego: What! Are you kidding? You aren't even a good writer.

True Self: It doesn't have to be a masterpiece. I could self publish.

Ego: So, who on earth would want to read your book?

True self: I will dedicate it to my children and it will be for them. The concepts will help them navigate life.

Ego: But they don't like hearing your spiritual talk. What makes you think they would read it?

True self: They might not. But it will be there for them if they change their mind. I will get extra copies made up for nephews, nieces, friends, and future generations.

Ego: Well you have a high opinion of yourself. Why on earth would they be interested in your story?

True self: Because it is just one example of an individual's journey into a more expanded awareness, which results in greater joy and peace. It may give them the courage and desire to go on their own journey.

Ego: I don't think they will get past the first line. You will bore them to tears.

True self: Maybe so. But this time Ego you are not going to beat me. I know you want me and my life to stay the same, so you can be the centre of attention. But get this. I am writing it anyway, because if nothing else, I will benefit from it. It will be a memoir to my amazing experiences and the lessons I have learned; a testament to the miracles that have occurred. So this time I am having the last say, and you can go and take a running jump!

Result

True self: 1
Ego: 0

Ok, so this scenario above is pretty much how my thinking went. One of my friends had been coercing me into writing a book for a few years. Every time I saw her, she would say "When is your book coming out?" I always replied that I wouldn't even know where to start. But clearly the Universe had other ideas for me. And it had to introduce the idea very gently. I started by thinking how my daughter would be going off to university in a year's time, and how lovely to be able to give her a gift that would help her navigate her way through life; a keepsake that she could refer to. And the answer was obvious. I would write a book, setting out the common spiritual thinking, with my experiences as a framework. Having more of an understanding of Universal Laws can help draw more positive experiences to yourself, and so this knowledge would be really beneficial. So, I started writing the book. But after writing a couple of chapters, I realised that this book was intended for more people than my daughter. Whereas this idea may have put me off initially, I was now happily immersed in it and enjoying myself too much to stop. My ego had been conquered.

Vanity

From the moment we are born, we enter a world where we are continuously brainwashed. We are told how to be and how to think, but it is so cleverly done, that we don't even recognise it. Our ego loves it, because the brainwashing exacerbates our insecurities.

The beauty industry is just one example of the millions made from our fears. The continuous bombardment of images portraying perfect and beautiful people, through newspapers, magazines, advertising and television, has resulted in a generation of young people obsessed with their looks and appearance; prepared to put themselves through dangerous cosmetic surgery, just to feel accepted and good about themselves. But the truth is this: real beauty comes from within. I have met old people who just radiate love and warmth; their inner light shines so bright – that I am blinded. This is true beauty, and unlike outer beauty, it withstands the test of time. It is eternal!

My personal experience with Ego

I suffered terrible shyness and lack of confidence when I was young. As a teenager I felt different to others and often felt inferior. I now understand that this was the ego taking control. It is just the opposite side of the spectrum to ego inflation. But the ego is still running the show, and is in desperate need of taming.

I have always been a horse lover, but the horse world is dominated by ego inflated people. The very nature of horse riding is such that the ego is harnessed and given free rein, from the desire of humans to dominate the horse, to the many competitions that a lot of human/horse partnerships attain to. As a child, I feasted on horse books; the majority which described competing in shows; winning that all important rosette, was the biggest motivation for owning a horse. I remember the excitement at winning my first rosette, when I was 14 years old, and sadly, I recall this better than the first day of owning my pony.

When I was young, dominance over the horse was all important. Articles advised that you must never let the horse have the last say; the horse is there to obey your every command, and his obedience is very much a reflection of your horsemanship skills.

Thankfully, attitudes are changing, but there is still a very long way to go. These days we are told that we must be a leader to our horse, but for most people, this is still very much along the lines of "the horse needs to be obedient and do as we ask."In essence therefore, this is not so different from previous thinking.

Not long after entering my spiritual phase of life, a beautiful and spirited thoroughbred named Jazz, came into my life. I always believe that we get the animals we need, and most are here to help in some way, or to teach a lesson. It was no coincidence that as I was learning to tame my ego, this horse came into my life to teach me that I had the heck of a long road to travel. Training this strong-minded mare, using conventional methods, was getting me nowhere. So I switched to more holistic methods; but surprisingly, I found these not a lot better, as the thinking was still based on being a leader to the horse. I knew in my heart of hearts, that my horse just wanted an equal partnership. And she wanted me to listen to her, as much as I was expecting her to listen to me. So, I threw all aims and ambitions out the window, and just listened. I acted on the information I received. The transformation in my horse was instant. She lost all her grumpiness and stopped planting and refusing to move. Finally, she was prepared to meet me half-way. I feel that I have learned far more from her, than she has from me. I do have to ask myself, who is training who?

So for me, being around horses has very much highlighted the destructive nature of the ego, to the point that it can really jeopardise the relationship between horse and human. I do believe that horses are just waiting for us to wake up and recognise this. They are trying to lead us out of our ego-centred natures, and into pastures new, where the human/horse bond will become more beneficial and enlightening for both.

This is just one example of how the ego can limit our experiences of life. In short, it wants to keep us small. The obsession with the "me" just leads to dissatisfaction with life, as we enter a rollercoaster of competition; getting the best jobs, the most money, the best car, the best house etc. Some people's lives become a meaningless round of trying to be one better than the neighbours. I have known such people. And were they happy? No. In fact, they were probably some of the saddest people I have met.

Taming the Ego

So, how do you go about taming the ego?

I have just read a good article on the internet by Cherie Dirksen. She has given some good tips on controlling the ego, so I have recreated them below:-

- *Do not take things personally. Be at peace with what others think about you. Not everyone will like you. Accept it, as we are always going to resonate with some people more than others.*

- *Think before you speak. Honour the power of your words and you will honour not only others, but also your sense of self. Choose your words wisely. People will pick up on this and return it in kind.*

- *Hold your tongue. The Ego loves to make itself right. But you can't force someone to see life through your eyes and perception. No, that is your ego trying to justify itself. Masters know when to speak, when to be silent and when their words will be like farting against thunder.*

- *Don't buy into the labels. Get in touch with who you really are and reconnect to your source. Look past the labels and identification that society plasters you with. You are a unique soul – find it through meditation.*

- *Quit comparisons. Learn to be comfy in your own skin. Fall in love with yourself and your uniqueness.*

- *Count your blessings. Try to see the positive aspects of your life and body.*

- *See divinity en masse. Don't try to elevate yourself above, or bury yourself below others. You are part of a collective consciousness of divine souls here on earth. See the divinity in yourself and others too. The ego won't be able to do this. To see the internal beauty in another, will put you on a level playing field.*

When you tame the ego, you are paving the way for a smooth and easy life flow. You relinquish judgements, comparisons and the need to be or feel superior. This is a frequency that you will project and as a result, people will be attracted to you. People who stand in their truth and integrity are like moths to a flame. Speaking from my own experience, it is hard work conquering the ego, and never a total accomplishment. I think it is a life-long commitment.

But it is worth doing, because it will make you a lot happier. You need to become extremely mindful to any negative thinking. And then try and look at it from a different perspective. This takes a lot of practice. It also takes a lot of love and compassion. But it can be done.

A man once told the Buddha, "I want happiness." The Buddha replied, "First remove "I" that's ego. Then remove "want", that's desire. And now all you are left with is happiness."

CHAPTER 5   ENERGY

Everything is made of energy. All living things are related intimately. If there is a war outside, there is a war inside. Because you have chosen the reality you live in.

Not so long ago, scientists were talking about finding the "Science of everything." Now, many of them admit that the more they learn, the more they realise they don't know. Consider for example, quantum physics, and the strange results of sub-atomic particles; that is, particles smaller than an atom. Early last century, experiments on the photon of light showed that sometimes it behaves like a particle, but it can also behave like a wave. Recently, experiments indicate that not only sub atomic particles, but even atoms can appear to be in two places at the same time and also follow different paths at the same time. Since everything is made up of atoms, the same laws therefore apply to the material world.

In short, everything is made up of energy; be it animal, plant, or object. Even our thoughts are energy. And this energy is in constant motion. I believe that energy never dies, but it can change form. I believe God, not to be a person, but more a loving energy that resides in everything: ourselves, animals, the grass, the sky. You name it, God is in it. This is what connects us all; that divine spark in each and every one of us.

I find it very easy to read people's energy and I always have done. I know instantly when I meet someone, before they have even opened their mouth, whether they can be trusted or not. In the same way, I find it just as easy to read an animal's energy. Through reading their energy, I know their personalities and characters. Now that I am conscious of it, I take it on myself, when I meet someone for the first time to read their energy. I can do this before they speak, and even when they are standing about 30 feet away. Sometimes, I can read very specific details about them. When I started my current employment, I was introduced to a man who I immediately pictured on the stage dressed as a dame. Some weeks later, he informed me that he was in an amateur dramatics group, and he had played the part of the dame in the Christmas pantomime. With another lady, I felt a very strong connection with Alzheimer's disease. After knowing her for about a year, she confided that both her parents suffered with the disease.

Places contain energy, usually the energy of the people who inhabited that space. Again, I have always been able to read the energy in houses. I used to drive my husband mad when we were house hunting for our first house. He would find a house he liked, only for me to turn around and say I didn't like the energy in the house. The same thing happened nine years ago, when we needed to move out of our house temporarily, while it was being extended. We viewed a house close by, with a prospect to rent. In every way it was ideal; close to our house, similar to our house, good price. But there was a problem. Although it was nicely decorated, and spotlessly clean, it had the most depressing energy. Once again, my husband had to bow down to my refusal to live in it. Happily, we went on to find a house that had lovely energy, and we spent a wonderful six months there.

Thoughts

Our thoughts carry tremendous energy. Every creation and everything we see, first originated as a thought. So we need to take responsibility for them. Thoughts are creative energy, and they carve, create and forge your future destiny. There is so much truth in the concept that reality is shaped by your thoughts. If you want harmony in your life, you must have harmony in your thoughts.

I can't stress enough, how important your thoughts are. They can keep you a prisoner, or they can set you free. It is very easy to get into a certain pattern of thinking, but if these thoughts are not serving you and are hindering you, it is very important to change your mindset. There are a lot of self-help books around at the moment, and these are very much centred round positive thinking and encouraging self-belief. Daily affirmations are also very useful.

It is very important to keep your thoughts focused on what you have, rather than what you don't have. If you are negative, and moan that the world is against you, you are sending out those beliefs into the universe, which responds by sending more negativity and bad luck your way. What you think, you attract. Think positively, because positive thinking is more in alignment with your soul. Negative thinking will just bring you confusion and bitterness.

A good habit to get into when you wake up in the morning is to create an intention and send that thought out with love. If you get into this routine, your life will start to change for the better.

Dr Masaru Emoto and his experiments with water crystals

Dr Emoto was able to prove with his water experiments, that thoughts and feelings affect physical reality. This Japanese scientist discovered that crystals formed in frozen water, reveal changes when specific, concentrated thoughts are directed towards them. Water exposed to loving thoughts and words, showed brilliant, complex and colourful snowflake patterns. In contrast, water exposed to negative thoughts, formed incomplete, asymmetrical patterns with dull colours.

Dr Emoto created a lot of photographs demonstrating his work, and these were published in his books, "Messages from water 1 and 2." His books were a huge success in Japan, and over 400,000 copies have been sold internationally. Following the publication of his book, he was called to lecture around the world and he has conducted live experiments in Japan, Europe and the U.S. His photos can be viewed on the internet.

The important message that Dr Emoto was trying to convey, was that our thoughts, attitudes and emotions as humans, deeply impact the environment, as well as each other. Since humans and the earth are composed mostly of water, we can affect others through our thoughts of them. The implications of this research create a new awareness of how we can positively impact the earth and our personal health.

Words

It isn't just our thoughts that carry energy, our words do too. Dr Andrew Newberg, a neuroscientist at Thomas Jefferson University, and Mark Waldman, a communications expert believe that changing your words can change your life. They wrote a book together, "Words can change your brain."

In their book, it is claimed that a single word can influence the expression of genes that regulate physical and emotional stress. When we use words like "love" and "peace" we can alter how our brain functions by increasing cognitive reasoning and strengthening areas in our frontal lobes. Using positive words rather than negative ones, can kick-start the motivational centres in the brain, propelling them into action. When we use negative words, we are preventing certain chemicals from being produced, and this contributes to stress management.

An excerpt from their book tells us how using the right words can literally change our reality. Holding a positive and optimistic word in your mind stimulates frontal lobe activity. Research has shown that the longer you concentrate on positive words, the more you begin to affect other areas of the brain. Functions in the parietal lobe start to change, which changes your perception of yourself and the people you interact with. A positive view of yourself, will bias you towards seeing the good in others, whereas a negative self-image, will make you more suspicious of others. Over time, the structure of your thalamus (an egg-shaped structure located deep in the centre of the brain) will also change in response to your conscious thoughts, words and feelings, and this affects the way you perceive reality.

Our words not only affect ourselves, they affect everyone around us. We all need to be more conscious of how powerful our words can be. They have tremendous healing power, but contrary to this, they can also be very damaging. A throw-away remark has the power to cause great upset to someone, and they can carry this wound around for years. I witnessed this recently. I had been invited to observe some Reiki attunements, and watched the healing they carried out on each other afterwards. It transpired that a lady had suffered a miscarriage about 30 or 40 years previously. A family member had remarked at the time that she should get over it, as it was only a baby. These words had caused her great upset and anger, and she had been carrying these feelings around ever since. Through the healing, she was able to release the emotions and let them go, forgiving the family member in the process. She also felt physical pain leave at the same time. As the tears rolled down her face, I realised with a jolt, how impactful our words can be. I promised myself to be fully conscious every time I opened my mouth, and to make sure that any words I utter come from a place of love.

Vibration

We are all responsible for the rate our energy vibrates. It is believed that someone who has a closed mind, or a negative and ungrateful mindset, has a lower energy vibration than someone who is positive and loving. The aim of the game is to raise your vibration, and we are all capable of doing this. Your energy vibration is not fixed. It is in a state of constant flux. It is impossible to live on earth and be positive, caring, loving and non-judgemental all the time. If we could achieve that, there would be no purpose for us being here, for there would be no lessons to learn. There are many ways to raise your vibration, such as: eating healthily, meditation, reading spiritual books or attending spiritual courses, listening to beautiful music, spending time with friends and family (those that are loving and supporting), doing good deeds and helping others; in other words, anything that opens your heart and connects you to love and joy. Emotions such as fear, anger, hate, jealousy, and judgemental thinking, lower your vibration.

At all times, we have a unique frequency signature that we emit out into the world. Compare yourself to a drop of water that falls into the centre of a still pond. The ripples it creates are unique vibrations that can be felt by you, the environment and others. When we are in alignment with our unique frequency or vibration, our physical form is supported, allowing emotional equilibrium and true passion to ignite our divine spark.

It is thought that metaphysical beings such as angels are all around us, but because their energy vibration is so much higher than our own, we can't see them.

This also applies to spirits. If we can increase our vibration, we have more chance of seeing and hearing them. This is possibly why children are more receptive to seeing spirits and angels. In their innocent and more loving state, their vibration is higher than us adults and this means they are more in tune with the invisible realms.

Increasing your vibrational energy will make you much happier and obviously this impacts also on the people around you and how they relate to you. If you meet a person who is smiling warmly, you are going to react much more favourably towards them than someone who is frowning at you. When we change our attitude towards others, then they change towards us. The last few years, I have really worked hard on improving my vibrational energy, and in the process I have noticed a big difference in how people relate to me. Wherever I go, people are bending over themselves to help and assist me. I think on an unconscious level we do sense the vibrational energy in others and react accordingly.

I had a very interesting experience recently that highlighted the impact of positive energy on a situation. I had gone into one of the banks to set up a standing order. There was only one man in front of me, so I thought "no problem. It shouldn't take long to sort." On the contrary, 15 minutes later, I was still standing there with this man in front of me. Now I regard patience as one of my virtues, but even I at this point, was starting to feel frustrated and fidgety. It was my work lunch break and I only get 30 minutes. It would mean having to stay later, to make my time up. As I glanced to the side, I noticed in the queue, a woman with her back to me. Tattooed across her back was a huge angel. I am not normally one for tattoos, but this one was beautiful and radiant. As I stared at it, I was instantly reminded to deal with this annoyance with a loving attitude. It was not the man's fault that he had something to sort that was taking all this time, and it was not the fault of the lady helping him. It was just one of those situations. I smiled as the message hit home, and I concentrated on keeping my feet still and sending out loving thoughts. Angels are such brilliant teachers! When the man finally finished sorting whatever it was that had taken so long, he turned around and thanked me sincerely for my patience. As did the lady behind the counter! I was actually surprised at how much appreciation they were passing on to me, just for my standing there. The energy between us was so beautiful, and made me feel great for the rest of the day.

When you vibrate with a higher energy, it is so uplifting and powerful. You feel that anything is possible. And of course, this energy gets passed on to everyone you come into contact with; family, friends, work colleagues, strangers. This ripple effect can be very far-reaching. You brighten up someone's day, which puts them in a good mood; they then help to uplift the energy of the people they come into contact with. We all impact on each other. So let's make it positive, rather than negative.

Auras

The human energy field is known as the aura. Within the aura, a person has seven subtle bodies of energy, all of which need to resonate in harmony with one another, creating balance in order to keep us in good health. Each of these bodies communicates with the next, passing on information in the form of energy. This energy travels through each layer or body until it reaches the physical body.

The aura acts as a two way receiver, connecting us to the energies around us. It senses the aura of other people, animals and objects that we are near. This then provides us with information on an intuitive level.

The auric field is very sensitive, and the aura can become drained and low in energy. Once it is weakened, holes appear which allow harmful energy to pass through, causing emotional imbalances, which eventually manifest into physical disorders and disease.

It is possible to see an aura with the naked eye, but some people have a greater ability to do this than others. With practise, I do believe that most of us can be trained to see them. There are also cameras available that pick up the colours of the auric field. A woman once showed me a picture of her aura, which had been specially taken. Amazingly, around the stomach area, there was a lot of bright light, and to the right of the picture there was a lot of pink. She was told that this had appeared because she was pregnant. The pink, pointed to her having a girl. This had been a shock to her, as she had no idea she was pregnant. She decided to carry out a pregnancy test, and to her amazement, it showed positive. She went on to have a girl, just as predicted.

Chakras

Throughout our bodies we have a flow of chi energy. This energy flows via the meridian lines, which pass through our organs, and round our body in one continuous flow. Along these meridian lines we have chakras.

Chakras are circular energy centres and they help us draw energy and light into our beings, and help us feel whole. They can become blocked, and are then unable to draw in the energy required to keep us in balance. These blockages arise from disharmony in our physical, emotional, mental and spiritual states. They can be released through healing, opening the chi energy source that is available.

It is very easy to get blockages. A few traumas or hurts in our life can do it, and blockages can also occur when we are not living our life purpose. It can make us feel unsettled and uneasy. The solution is to change our lives and get back on track.

There are seven main chakra points in the body. I do not intend going into detail here, but if you want to find out more, then I suggest you look on the internet. Each chakra has a colour corresponding to it, and each one, represents certain characteristics.

When I first learned about chakras, I discovered that my throat chakra was very blocked, so I did a lot of work to release this blockage. In doing so, it has made a huge difference. Whereas at one time, I felt very uncomfortable talking to people I didn't know, now I often initiate conversations with strangers. Also, I now find it much easier to talk my truth and not worry about what people may think.

I can't emphasize enough how important it is to clear any blocked chakras. In doing so, it can literally change your life.

Death

When we die, our energy leaves our body, and transfers. We become a soul without a body. I never believed in the idea of heaven and hell, because I believe in a loving God, not a judgemental one.

Those who have behaved badly on earth cause their own hell by torturing themselves with the realisation that they have wounded others.

The accounts of NDE's do seem to bear this belief out. As do the accounts of mediums. Whilst writing this, I read about a lady who had been deeply wounded by the abuse that was inflicted on her as a young child by a family member. She attended a mediumship evening at her local spiritualist church, and was deeply affected by the message passed on to her by the medium. The abuser who had long since passed over, came through, and expressed his deep sorrow for what he had put her through. He begged for her forgiveness. The woman had never told anyone what she had gone through, so for her, it was undeniable proof that the afterlife is real. In fact, she was so affected by this she is now training to be a medium herself, because she totally understands how this work can make a massive difference to peoples' lives.

It is my belief, based on everything I have read on the subject, that your thoughts create your death, in the same way they create your life. So if you can see the good and beauty in others and in the world, then this is what you are likely to see when you die. The rate you are vibrating at when you die is a great indicator of the life you will experience in death. It is said that some people's vibration is so low, that they are unable to see the spirits and angels that have come for them, and they are unable to see and move towards the light. This is why so many spirits fail to cross over successfully; instead they are stuck in that in between state, where they still believe they are alive. This may last until some enlightened and spiritual person makes contact, helping to move them into the light.

After you pass over, it is my belief that a review is carried out of your life, where you see everything that has transpired; good or bad. No judgement is made, but you are clearly able to see which lessons you failed and which were successful. This then helps you decide, whether to reincarnate again, or whether to spend time in heaven, healing and learning there. Although you are in spirit, you can still see each other in body form, and there are beautiful buildings and landscapes; space and time as we understand it do not exist. You can be anywhere you want, just with the power of thought, and everyone communicates through telepathy. This is comforting if you have lost a child, because you know that your soul is already with them in the future, if that is where they choose to be.

In western society, death is a pretty taboo subject. Particularly if someone dies young, we see it as the ultimate tragedy, and our grief can be terrible. We fail to see that quality of life is more important than quantity. And we fail to recognise that we all come into this life, having already decided when we will die. Sometimes people remember, like my friend Jon, who always knew that he was not going to make 30. He died when he was 29.

When I was 20, my beloved dog, Candy passed over. I was devastated, because she had been with us, since I was 7 years old, and she was part of the family. For years I dreamed about her, and the dream was always the same. I would be overjoyed to see her and would state "You didn't really die. It was just a dream." And that was the point she was always making, and which I failed to see for a long time; the point being that she hadn't really died. She had just transitioned, and in spirit she was still with us. When I finally did get this, she stopped appearing in my dreams. For now I know that one day we will all be together again.

This leads me on to my next point. It is my belief that you always stay with the same soul family, through all the different lifetimes, be it that you may be connected in different ways. So for example, a mother and son in this lifetime, may have had a role reversal in a previous lifetime, or may have even been husband and wife. The soul family supports us in all our different roles, and helps us to grow, evolve and learn our lessons. A recent lesson I have learned is this: when a soul is determined to spend time with you on the earthly plane, it will find a way to be with you, even if that means it comes back into an animal's body. This lesson surprised me, because I had always believed that you came back in the same type of body i.e. a human remained human through all their incarnations. But having given it a great deal of thought, why should you not come back in a different form. We are all connected after all, and with the divine, there are simply no limitations. Anything is possible! Also, because time does not exist in the spiritual plane, a soul can choose to come back to an earlier time period from when they died.

I think that we all need to be able to talk about death much more than we do. My husband can't understand my interest in it, and thinks it is morbid and depressing. But I totally disagree. The more you understand about death, the less you fear it, and the more you can understand life. I now see death as a really beautiful transition into another way of being. Those people who have had near death experiences have come back to life with a completely different perspective. The fear has gone, and is replaced with a beautiful unconditional love; something they seem able to have brought back from heaven. They find their lives have been transformed completely by the experience and they live with a lot more love, joy and purpose than they ever did before. In short, they are living heaven on earth.

Horses and energy

I feel that we have a long way to go in fully understanding energy. It seems that there is a lot to be discovered and understood. At the moment, there still seems to be a huge gap in our knowledge. As a Reiki healer and animal communicator, I am very much aware of energy, and I can certainly feel the changes in energy, but I by no means fully understand how the processes work.

Horses seem to be very sensitive to energy, and read our energy effortlessly. I often work on the ground with my horse, and we play with energy. It fascinates me how my horse responds so well to the energy in my body. So when I want her to move forwards in a quicker pace, I build the energy up in my body, and then drop the energy when I want her to slow down. In a session, after about 30 minutes, we are so in tune with each other that I only have to think what I want her to do, for her to do it. It is truly magical, when you get to this point. I actually believe that we have a lot more to learn, before we can catch up with the horse's understanding of energy.

In the next chapter, I discuss how we can use energy in a positive way, to draw better things to ourselves.

CHAPTER 6   THE LAW OF ATTRACTION AND KARMA

Abundance is not something we acquire,
It is something we tune into.

Wayne Dyer

The Law of attraction is a very important universal law, but I have to confess that I had never even heard of it until a few years ago. I wish more people were aware of it, and fully understood the power it can exert over us. When you have a full understanding, you can use it to create the life you truly desire.

Awareness of the concept has been around for thousands of years. There are numerous references to it in the New Testament, and scholars and authors such as Shakespeare, made reference to it in some of their works. It has recently gained popularity as a result of the book "The secret" written by Rhonda Byrne. When it was published in 2006, it became a huge bestseller, and now the practice has been adopted by most leading spiritual thinkers. There are literally thousands of people out there who claim that the success and abundance in their life, is down to understanding and adopting the principles of the Law of Attraction.

The principles

In essence, the belief behind the law is very simple; what you give out in the universe is what you get back. So if you are happy, positive and loving, then you attract these things to yourself. If on the other hand, you are miserable and negative, then you just attract more bad things.

This doesn't mean to say that bad things don't happen to positive, happy people. They do. And I think this is possibly because of other laws that take precedence over The Law of Attraction, such as our life lessons, and the Law of Karma.

Generally, when I observe life, I can see the law in operation. There is someone I know who is incredibly joyful and happy. She seems permanently to radiate the most intense positivity. And guess what? She is having a ball. Her life is full of fantastic and life enhancing opportunities. Her life very much reflects the person she is. Some people might read this and say, "Well that is why she is so happy. She has a fantastic life, so she has something to be happy about." But I don't think that is the case. Her very essence is a joyful radiant being, and I believe that her soul acts as a magnet, and draws all the beautiful stuff in life to her. So she attracts the ideal partner, the fulfilling job, perfect opportunities. It is not luck.

Some people may unconsciously use the law to their advantage, as they may naturally be loving, joyful people. Others may use it consciously. I do know someone who used the law to find her ideal husband. She made a list of all the qualities she wanted in a husband, and then asked the Universe to find him for her. She visualised her future life, married to this man. He materialised, and they are now happily married.

How to attract abundance into your life

These steps will help you attract more abundance into your life:-

- *Visualise what exactly it is that you want in your life. Be very clear what you want. Write it down, possibly in a note to the universe. Thank the universe for receiving it, for you must imagine that you have already received it. You may also wish to create a visualisation board somewhere in the house, where you can pin things that you wish to manifest, like a holiday destination or new house. This is then a constant reminder to the universe, that this is what you wish to draw to yourself.*

- *Imagine very clearly in your mind what it is you wish to manifest, using all your senses; sight, hearing, touch, smell and imagine the feeling of joy when you receive your wish. For example, if it is a house, imagine what it looks like, how it smells, the noises around it, and how it feels when you touch it. Picture yourself walking through the door for the first time, knowing that this is your new home. Feel the excitement and anticipation.*

- *Be very grateful for what you have received. Gratitude is very important, so I have discussed this separately below.*

- *Be careful of any blocks that you may have in your thinking. These may prevent things manifesting. For example, a lot of people have a negative relationship with money. We have all heard and probably used the phrase "Money is the root of all evil." Well actually it isn't. The problem isn't with the money. Like pretty well anything in life, money can be used for good, or it can be used for not so good. The fault isn't with the money. It is with the humans and their attitude towards money.*

- *Also, some people block themselves off from receiving financial abundance, by believing they are not worthy, or by feeling guilty. They may see desiring money as being greedy. There are others worse off than themselves, so why should they wish for more money. This is selfish, right? Well no, it isn't. We think there is only so much to go around. But this isn't true. Abundance is all around you. Your soul is actually a magnet to it, and the universe wants to bestow abundance on you all the time. Of course, it is important what you do with it when you get it.*

- *Develop a good relationship with receiving. Tell yourself that you are deserving, and you have a right to abundance as much as the next person.*

- *Be willing to give unconditionally. Give love and joy to everyone else, for this is what will then be given to you.*

Be aware that if you are putting all these steps into place, but you still feel that you are not getting what you asked for, there may be a good reason for this. It may not be in alignment with your soul purpose, or the path you are supposed to follow. I have learned that when you are on the right path, there is a real flow and momentum. Things seem to happen

91

effortlessly and quickly. The right people come into your life at the right time, and opportunities and great advice just falls straight into your lap. It all starts to feel very magical. If you are on the wrong path, however, and the direction you are taking is not really going to serve your soul, everything feels like an uphill struggle. You face obstacle after obstacle, with no end in sight. If you ever feel this in your life, please just take time out to consider the possibility that this might not be the right path for you. With practise, this becomes easier. It is just being conscious to what is happening. When you recognise those roadblocks, you can do something to change them. Consider changing your direction and then see what happens.

The last few years I have really fancied myself as a horse trainer. With my understanding of horses' minds and animal communication skills, I imagined myself being able to transform my horse. People on the yard would see this amazing transformation, and would ask me to work with their own horses. I could then pass the same skills on to other people. To achieve this, I also tried to learn everything about the horse's natural asymmetry. I learned groundwork, lunging and In hand skills and I took a course in Straightness training. Although what I learned was incredibly valuable, I was still no closer to attaining my goal. My horse became slightly more supple, and able to take the weight better on her hindquarters, but our progress was limited to say the least. Not only that; she was becoming increasingly grumpy. Then one day I heard her say, "This is all wrong. You are supposed to be using my mind not my body. We are healers, not riders or trainers." Although it was a bolt from the blue, I knew deep in my heart that she was right. As soon as I recognised this fact, everything started to flow magically. I received so many signs that I was on the right path that it almost felt like I had entered an altered reality. You can read the full story in the chapter, "I believe in Unicorns."

Gratitude

This is a very important concept in its own right and does tie in with the Law of Attraction. Basically, the more grateful you are for the things in your life, the more you will receive.

As a child I loved the Walt Disney film, "Pollyanna". It is about a young girl, who is able to recognise the positive in everything. She loves playing "The glad game." Through her upbeat and radiant nature, she not only draws happiness to herself, but she changes the lives of the people around her. One old lady sheds her embittered attitude and deep unhappiness, eventually learning to love this young girl. Although I had absolutely no concept of the Law of Attraction whilst watching this film, the workings of this law are very much in evidence. I could never understand, why, as children, we were not taught more about positivity and gratitude. The film so clearly demonstrates how much easier your life can be if you adopt such forms of energy.

Even the bible touches on aspects of this Law. In her book "The magic" Rhonda Byrne draws attention to a passage from the Gospel of Matthew.

"Whoever has will be given more, and he will have an abundance. Whoever does not have, even what he has will be taken from him."

Rhonda explains that this passage has mystified, confused, and been misunderstood by people over the centuries. When you first read the passage, it appears unjust, as it seems to be saying that the rich will get richer and the poor will get poorer. But, Rhonda reckons there is a missing word: gratitude.

"Whoever has gratitude will be given more, and he will have an abundance. Whoever does not have gratitude, even what he has will be taken from him."

For anyone wanting to appreciate and practise feeling gratitude, I would really recommend Rhonda's book, "The Magic." I found the exercises in the book extremely beneficial. I always felt I was a pretty appreciative person, but this book really opened my eyes to the things in life we take for granted. If you carry out the exercises religiously, on a daily basis (they only take a few minutes first thing on the morning and last thing at night) you will really see your life start to change. Towards the end of the book, there was an exercise where you thanked the universe for the good news you received that day. It got to about 9.00pm at night, and I was sitting there thinking "No good news received yet. This exercise hasn't worked." Ten minutes later a friend texted me, congratulating me on winning some healing beads, a competition I had entered on Facebook. The funny thing was, I hadn't even entered a competition. I had liked a healer's page, and it transpired that this was enough for me to win these beads. Those beads proved particularly beneficial. My daughter's pony had developed a really strange habit when being ridden, of sticking his head up and out. The vet had failed to get to the bottom of it, and over the six weeks of the problem manifesting, it had worsened. But as soon as we attached the beads to the bridle, the problem just disappeared.

The Law of Karma

When a bird is alive.... it eats ants
When the bird is dead... ants eat the bird
Time and circumstances can change at any time.
Don't devalue or hurt anyone in life
You may be powerful today
But remember
Time is more powerful than you!
One tree makes a million match sticks
Only one match stick needed to burn a million trees
So be good, and do good.

Yes, I think most people are aware of how karma works. "What goes around, comes around," is the general thinking about karma.

The karmic laws are very important. When we understand them and act on them, we can start to grow and evolve. We can create good karma, by doing good deeds, being kind and thoughtful, or we can create bad karma, by being the opposite. It is the law of cause and effect, and you deserve everything that happens to you, good or bad. In this way, you create your own happiness and misery. One day you will be in the same circumstances that you put someone else in. In other words, it is your actions that create your future.

There was a really good example of instantaneous karma recently in the news. A man was on the train, when another man, rudely pushed past him. When he asked him what on earth he thought he was doing, he was subject to being sworn at. Later on in the day, the man on the train was getting ready to interview someone, when guess who should turn up? The interviewee was the rude man on the train. That would be one interview he wished he hadn't turned up for.

People often think that when others are behaving badly, that they are getting away with it. The phrase, "It doesn't pay to be honest" is so often bandied about. Well actually, it does pay to be honest, because there is always payback. It may not be in this lifetime, it might be in the next, but it will most certainly happen. So the abuser in this life may come back as the abused in the next life. You do have to be careful here though, because it doesn't mean that every disadvantaged or suffering person in this life has bad karma which they are working off. There may be other reasons why their soul has chosen to undergo suffering; such as teaching a lesson to someone, or trying to create a change in the law. It is reckoned that the whales that are beaching themselves are doing so to draw attention to their plight. They have volunteered to come to earth and to go through this to make humans aware of what we are doing to the environment. There may be a connection with offshore wind farms, and whales beaching. It is thought that the noise is affecting the sonar of the whale, leaving them vulnerable to coming close to shore. So these whales have volunteered to go through this, to educate us humans on responsibility and accountability.

The Law of Karma encourages you to make conscious choices that nourish others and yourself, leading to healing for everyone concerned.

CHAPTER 7   ANIMAL WISDOM

It is just like man's vanity and impertinence
To call an animal dumb
Because it is dumb to his dull perceptions.

Mark Twain

You may wonder why I have included a chapter on animals in a spiritual book, but I believe that animals can contribute hugely to our spiritual journey. Not only that. I think they can evolve our very souls. They certainly have in mine. I really think that animals are God's gift to man. You only have to think of the many ways that animals have served us over the years to recognise this. And this service goes way beyond providing food and clothing. Even now, in this technological age, animals are serving us in countless ways. In addition to this, as pets, their ability to love us unconditionally is a huge blessing and comfort. The human-companion animal bond (HCAB) is a recognised term that looks at the bonds and benefits of having animals in our lives. Not only do they provide companionship, but they help increase social interaction and improve the owner's health and well-being. Their qualities and outlook on life can offer us many lessons, and very importantly, they encourage us to open our hearts. There is so much they can teach us. I consider some of the most popular animals below, and the roles they play in our lives, but in truth, every species of animal has something to teach us.

Dogs

I think that dogs have really lived up to the statement as "man's best friend." They have been by our side for thousands of years, and in that time they have been the most willing of partners. The roles they have taken on are too numerous to mention, but through their actions they have proven beyond doubt to be extremely brave, noble and humble. And for millions of people, dogs have been a lifeline, serving them in ways that have enabled them to live independently. This is particularly true of guide and service dogs. Many charities exist today that pair specially trained dogs with people who have disabilities. "Dogs for Good" is one such charity, with their dogs helping to normalise people's lives in many ways. Children with autism for example, often become calm and focussed when they have a companion dog to help them with everyday tasks.

Living with a dog is a wonderful experience. A dog that has been loved and well cared for returns unparalleled unconditional love and devotion. If you treat a dog with respect, you can practically guarantee a truly joyful partnership. It's fantastic when you come home after a hard day's work, to be met by a fur ball of love, wagging his tail furiously and leaping around you in excitement. There is no better welcome. When you are down and sad, a dog will know instinctively how you are feeling. He will push his nose into your face, his message so clear from his eyes; "Don't worry. I am here for you." They are incredibly intuitive and I don't doubt they can read minds. I know a woman whose dog kept nudging her and intently sniffing a particular area on her body. She felt this was out of character, so went to see her doctor. She was diagnosed with cancer. Fortunately it was caught in the early stages, and thanks to her dog, she went on to make a full recovery. She owed him her life.

Whatever the size of a dog, they have a massive heart and they wish to be our protectors, both in the physical and spiritual world. A friend recognises that one of her animal spirit guides is her deceased Rhodesian Ridgeback (see the chapter on "The Dark Side" for this story).

When I look into a dog's eyes, I am always moved by the love and compassion staring back at me. How anyone can neglect or abuse these beautiful animals is beyond me. When I was about sixteen I was walking across a field on the way to see my pony. There was a puppy sitting dejectedly on her own, in the middle of the field, right in my pathway. As I looked down at this dog, her eyes bore deeply into my soul. For as long as I live I will never forget the look that dog gave me. She was pleading with her heart and soul for me to help her. This was the first time in my life that I was consciously aware that an animal was "talking" to me, and I could hear her clearly. She had been abandoned and was in desperate need of help. After such a heartfelt plea for help, I did what came naturally. I scooped her up in my arms, cuddled her, and told her that she could come home with me. When I put her back down, she was a changed dog. Gone, the sad, hang dog expression. She was bouncing around me with joy and excitement. Gleefully, she accompanied me to the stables to turn my pony out, before returning home with me for some much needed food, water and sleep. Sadly, we weren't able to keep her, as our dog would not tolerate another dog in the house and was overwhelmed by jealousy, but my friend's mum took her on and she went on to have a wonderful life with her. How people can abandon dogs, or any animal come to that, I just don't know.

Sitting on a beach, I do enjoy watching the dogs at play. They always appear to be so, so happy. They really teach us how to connect to joy and that inner child inside ourselves. And they are so forgiving, and never, ever judge us. Oh, to love and play like a dog! For me, dogs are true earth angels.

Cats

Cats are very different to dogs. They are more independent, more discerning and definitely more proud, but they still have the same love to offer, although this is reserved for the select few. They certainly have a preference, and tend to choose us, rather than us choosing them.

As with dogs, they can offer a lifeline to people. I enjoyed the book and film, "A street cat named Bob." This is based on the true story of a cat coming into the life of a man and saving him from a life of drug taking and living rough on the streets. He compares this cat to an angel. I have also heard of cats who have helped autistic children. There is a young girl, Iris Grace who is severely autistic and a very talented painter. She is best friends with her cat, who accompanies her everywhere – on her bike, in the bath, swimming, and sits faithfully over her when she paints. Watching the video of them together, you see a beautiful union that is almost otherworldly. This Maine coon cat has even helped overcome the little girl's fear of water. He is described as Iris's "guardian angel" and watching them together, you can't dispute the fact that this cat is her lifeline. The videos can easily be found on the internet and are well worth watching.

I do think cats have an awareness superior to our own, and they are quite psychic. Someone once told me they were cleaning out the bathroom, when their cat appeared in the doorway, screaming at them. Eventually, they could stand the noise no longer, and so walked towards the cat to move him away. As they did so, a huge cabinet fell off the wall, right where they had been standing. If the cat hadn't moved her away, it would have crashed straight onto her head, and possibly killed her. This woman was in absolutely no doubt whatsoever that this cat had saved her from a serious injury. And she was convinced that the cat did so knowingly.

Horses

Horses are the shamans of the animal world; they are just so spiritual. It is natural for them to regularly zone out of the physical world, through the many naps they take. Just watching them galloping along freely, with their flowing manes and tails is enough to take my breath away. They are so majestic, beautiful and powerful, but at the same time, so gentle and humble. They are the masters of contradiction!

I have spent a lifetime around horses, but they never cease to amaze me. The more I get to know them, the more there is to get to know. My first touch of a horse, at about four years old, is seared on my memory, and nothing will erase it. I still recall being enthralled by this beautiful, glossy, chestnut horse, standing in front of me. The sight of him took my breath away, and the touch of his coat was like silk. I had never touched anything that felt so exquisite. It was the start of an enduring love affair!

Horses have an incredible ability to pick up on our deepest feelings and emotions. They are able to uncover things about us that we have buried deep inside. Not only do they uncover them, but they reveal them to us and ask us to deal with them. This is why equine therapy is taking off to such a degree in the 21st century. Now that we have recognised this ability in the horse, we have created a completely new role for them. Anyone doubting this ability should read my awakening account in chapter 1. And from this experience I learned something even more amazing about them; that they have the ability to be really great healers. There is a centre in Canada (Equinisity) where this trait is fully utilised. People go there to be healed by horses. People are rolled out on tables, and the horses meditate and carry out healing over them. The results are supposedly so good, that there is worldwide interest. I think that these healing centres will become more common as we proceed through this century, and continue to recognise these amazing abilities in the horse.

I believe that horses can awaken that latent spirituality in us. My horse Tiffany, who I wrote about in the first chapter, was I believe, very psychic, and through our connection, was able to share her ability with me. We had some amazing things happen over the years, compounded by the fact that Tiffany always acted like she understood everything I said to her. I could give her really complex instructions verbally, and she would obey them to the letter. She also had this amazing ability to sense whether we were going on a short ride, or whether it was going to be a bit of a trek. If the former, she would jog from the off. If the long ride however, she would pace herself beautifully, and there was no jogging. She always knew! One winter, I had torn my neck muscles, and was finding it very difficult to lift my arms to put the headcollar and bridle on. Not a problem when Tiffany was around though. She would just put her head very low to the ground, making it really easy for me. Her ability to read me, never failed to amaze me.

It is my belief that horses are leading us out of our ego-centred natures, where we are the herd leader; dominant and demanding. Instead they are revealing a new path; a path that only appears, when we have overcome and conquered our ego. This is the path to true partnership, connection and freedom; for both horse and trainer/rider. And this is far more fulfilling than anything that has ever come before. For through this connection, both horse and rider/trainer can find true power and fulfilment. We just need to recognise the powerful wisdom, mirroring back to us through our horses' eyes. They have much to teach us!

Linda Kavanagh has written some fantastic books about horses, which take you into a different world; more a dreamscape. Her journey into this altered reality, eventually concluded with her setting up an equine assisted therapy centre in America, where she has used horses' powers of perception, combined with their healing abilities, to help thousands of abuse victims and emotionally wounded people. As she delved deeper into the knowledge she was tapping into, she also discovered that horses have the perfect leadership qualities. She has since gone on to write a book about how horses can teach us all we need to know about being the ideal leader.

Dolphins

Dolphins are well-known for their high intelligence. But I also believe, they are also highly spiritual, with many lessons to teach us.

Stories abound of dolphins' natural affinity with man. They reach out to us, happy to connect with us, play and swim alongside us. And there are many stories of their heroic nature, saving humans and leading them away from danger.

They are naturally joyful and playful, and with these qualities, they connect us to our inner child. They are also very community orientated, understanding that they can achieve so much more when they work together. I have seen videos of pods of dolphins working together to catch large shoals of fish; their ingenuity and intelligence is acutely evident, as is their extraordinary ability to work together as a team; each having a part to play, and instinctively knowing where to position themselves and when to act. A work of genius!

They are natural nurturers and healers. According to marine biologists there is something about the vibrational energy of a dolphin and its sonar that has an effect on our bio-molecular structure. Dolphins can break up negative energy, and help us to feel more at peace, harmonious and well. This may explain why we all have that innate desire to swim with dolphins. And those lucky enough to have had the opportunity recognise it as an incredibly intense and amazing experience.

More than anything, the dolphin teaches us about forgiveness. We treat this beautiful creature so abominably; they get caught in our nets, we deprive them of food, pollute their sea, and keep them captive in small pools for our entertainment. The barbaric annual dolphin hunts are heartbreaking beyond words. But in spite of this, the dolphin never gives up on us and still offers to connect with us. They are true spiritual teachers. If only we listened and followed their example.

My dolphin vision

I am in absolutely no doubt that dolphins are highly spiritual beings who are here to provide us with wisdom. As a child, I was fascinated with dolphins, and would have loved to have been able to swim and interact with them. Although this opportunity never arose, I have been lucky enough to have received a message from them.

For about a week, I had been procrastinating on our cruelty to animals. Although the internet can be a great source of information, at times it can seem quite depressing – highlighting animal cruelty cases, and the many ways we betray an animal's trust. All week, I had been raging against the unfair treatment of animals, and it had reached a point where I just didn't feel I could regard myself as part of the human race. It was just breaking my heart.

On the Saturday I had attended a Reiki workshop. As is usual, the energy was beautiful and I felt my vibrational energy had heightened. When I awoke on the Sunday morning, before I opened my eyes, a picture started to materialise. The darkness in front of my eyes was like a palette. Very slowly, a picture was being coloured in and was starting to take form. It was as if the universe had taken a light green colouring pen, and was creating this picture. During the process, I just couldn't believe what I was witnessing. I knew I was awake and this was no dream. The finished picture was of two dolphins, rearing out the water and facing each other. As I took this in, I also heard the words "yin and yang," sounding in my head. I knew this was a clear message, but I had no idea what it meant.

To decipher the meaning of the vision, I looked initially on the internet and was instantly drawn to an article, proclaiming that dolphins embody the meaning of "yin and yang." Dolphin meaning is connected with the themes of duality; fish and mammal; sea animal and air-breather; joyful and serious. And this "yin and yang" embodiment is evident by the amount of dolphin jewellery with this design theme. I also meditated on the meaning, and the explanation was thus:

Duality is an inescapable part of physical life. The human condition in itself is one of duality. Love and hate are part of human nature. There will always be cruelty in the world, because every man who walks the earth embodies a shadow side. There is no escaping human nature. But look to the dolphin, who are masters of duality. See how they are capable of great joy. Connect to this joy, and like them, don't take life too seriously. Also, like the dolphin, embody love and forgiveness. Accept what is and remember there has to be balance. Everything is in perfect and divine order. The colour green also represents healing, so be healed by this vision.

Butterflies

I told a lot of people about my spiritual awakening at the time it occurred, and a surprising number of people told me similar stories, where they believed their departed loved one had made contact with them. A fair number of these stories involved butterflies. I heard about the butterfly who sat on the coffin the whole way through the funeral service. Then there was the butterfly who sat on somebody's hand the whole way through the funeral service. Another butterfly came to rest on someone's hand every day for a week, after the death of her sister. All the stories recounted to me were along these lines. And since then, I have discovered through the books I have read, that butterflies are a common sign to see, following the death of a loved one. In fact Theresa Cheung, whose books are based on the stories that people send in to her, claims to have received an awful lot of letters from funeral directors who have noticed a lot of butterflies present at funerals, and recount stories similar to those mentioned above.

So why is this? I think the answer is twofold. Firstly, they are perhaps a winged messenger, sent by the angels, to comfort a person and reassure them that the soul of their departed loved one lives on. Or the departed could be using the energy of that butterfly, to say goodbye to a loved one and to comfort them in their hour of need. They may even have transferred some of their soul essence into the butterfly. The butterfly is a wonderful reminder that just when we think our life is done, we transform into something far more magnificent and beautiful. Are the dead just trying to tell us that their transformation is complete, and they are living on in a different, more wonderful form?

Whether you believe or not, there is no denying that the butterfly can teach us a great deal. The magnificent life of the butterfly closely mirrors the process of spiritual transformation, as we each have the possibility of being reborn through going within. By retreating into our inner being, and surrounding ourselves with prayer, meditation, spiritual books and courses, we are ready at some point to emerge and be reborn into a new way of being.

The butterfly with its magnificent and short life, also reminds us to enjoy the here and now.

Birds

In a similar way to the butterfly, birds can also be winged messengers from the spirit world. On a couple of occasions, I have really felt this to be true.

I was partaking in an animal communication course and we were encouraged to do readings on each other's animals. The woman who carried out a communication on my horse Jazz, mentioned that she had a white dove as a spirit guide. The very next day when I was up the yard, Jazz was tied to a metal bar in the middle of the barn. But what completely shocked me was this; she had a white dove walking around her feet. Just incredible! The white dove remained on the yard for about six months. In that time, we all became quite fond of it, and it did seem to bring a sense of peace and calm on to the yard. Then one day, as suddenly as he arrived, he was gone.

I have a friend who often puts a picture of a robin on her Facebook page, with the message "When a robin constantly visits you or crosses your path; a loved one in heaven is trying to say Hello! I'm with you." This summer, for a period of five days, whenever I was up the yard, there was a robin who would hardly leave my side. Sometimes, he would be with me for about an hour. I would be mucking out, and he would be sitting in the wheelbarrow. One time, there were a few of us talking in a group, and he just sat in the middle of us. No-one could believe their eyes. On the fifth day, I decided that he was so tame, I would take some of the horses feed in my hand, and see if he would take it. I held my hand out, and amazingly, he flew over my hand before diving in and taking the food. He did this on the morning and on the night. I was beside myself with happiness; it was such a beautiful experience. But then he was gone; never to be seen again. Like the dove, he had disappeared as quickly as he appeared.

I thought no more of it, until I was writing my Christmas cards. I was using my address book, which is about thirty years old. For no reason at all, I suddenly started thinking of the robin. And suddenly,

I was feeling a connection with him and my friend Jon, who had died 20 years previously. I became aware of an inner knowing; that if I looked at his address in my book, it would provide proof of this connection. I hurriedly looked up his address. I focused on the words Woodruff Close, wondering whether ruff could relate to the red breast. But it was the next line that I should have been looking at. The name Robinswood couldn't have been a clearer connection!

The power animal (spirit guide or totem animal)

Shamans recognise the spiritual value of animals, and the lessons they can teach us. They often invoke a spirit animal to accompany them on their shamanic, ceremonial journeys into the invisible realms.

But we all have spirit guide animals, even though we may be unconsciously aware of them. It is said that some spirit animals are always with us, and others appear, as and when we have lessons to learn or messages to listen to. When I learned to meditate, I recognised that a big red fox kept appearing in my meditations. I was also reminded of the fact that in my early twenties, I used to school my horse on some parkland, which was lit up at night. One winter, a fox appeared every time I schooled, sitting on the outer edge of the circle, only to slink off, when I had finished schooling. I always found the appearance of this fox a great comfort, and felt protected; there did feel a spiritual connection between us. So reflecting on this, it was not really surprising to find that a fox has always been my spirit guide. If a fox is your totem animal, you embody qualities of intense loyalty and the ability to be able to think outside the box. You are also good at blending in and remaining unnoticed in company, as well as caring about people and being sensitive to their feelings. And yes, I can relate to all this.

My other totem animal is the eagle owl. The night before I was attuned to Reiki 1, my Native American spirit guide, Kali, appeared in a meditation. On his shoulder, sat a beautiful huge eagle owl, and I learned that as well as the fox, he is also my permanent animal guide. The eagle, as a totem animal, teaches us that we have the ability to soar to great heights, if only we can find the courage to do so. Eagle people are often seen apart from the crowd, where their perspective can give them a better view of the big picture. People, who have the owl as a totem, discover wisdom in the silence. They can also see the spiritual being inside the body, and can usually see what is hidden to most. It gives you the ability to see the true reality beyond the illusion and deceit. The owl also offers the inspiration and guidance necessary to deeply explore the unknown and the magic of life. Again, I can relate to all of this. As an introvert, I tend to draw information from feelings and the inner voice, and I am really good at assessing people's character and personality. I have always been able to see through the mask. And my interest in the unknown has been a lifelong fascination.

Interestingly, all the quizzes I have done on Facebook, which reveal your spirit animal, have always come up with either the fox or owl. The questions were all to do with character and personality traits, so there was no way of knowing the result. Fascinating, particularly as I only joined Facebook after knowing my spirit animals, so I certainly wasn't influenced by the results.

Recently, the goose has been grabbing my attention. The geese are making their journey to warmer climes. Frequently, I have heard their call and I look into the sky to watch them fly directly overhead. And this is the weird thing. Their flight is always directly over my head and the number of birds in the flock are growing. Today, on hearing their call, I looked into the sky. This time they weren't heading straight for me. But then something very strange happened. The flock broke into two groups, and the larger group changed direction slightly. And guess what? They flew straight over my head, and then rejoined the other group. "Ok" I thought, "I need to look up the symbolism of the goose." It would appear that geese are very protective of each other. If in flight, one gets injured, another goose will always stay with it. They are never left alone. So there is a message here that I am protected. Also, geese in flight can signify that you are finding or nearing your purpose in life, that which gives you bliss. Again, this makes sense. I am realising my spiritual purpose and my path is becoming increasingly clear. I feel that the geese are telling me that I am on the right path, and I just need to keep pressing forward; the golden egg awaits.

So, start taking notice of the animals that appear in your life. For example if a deer crosses your path, check what this means. If you dream of an animal, find out what this represents. The joy of the internet, is that we only have to press a few buttons, and these things are revealed to us. You will soon come to realise that there is a whole world of wisdom out there, which is trying to communicate with us.

Harmony with the natural world

One of the saddest things about living in a modern western society, is that we have become so separated from the natural world. In so doing, our treatment of animals is quite shocking. Horror stories abound: animal experimentation, backyard breeding, intensive factory farming, trophy hunting, poaching; to name just a few. We consider ourselves evolved beings, but our treatment of animals is no reflection of an evolved race. We have such a long way to go. In fact, indigenous tribes are far kinder and appreciative of animals. They may still hunt them for food, but when they kill them, it is done with total reverence and appreciation. They bless the animal for giving up its life. They recognise the animal to be a beautiful, intelligent and sentient being, with a soul. So why have we lost sight of this? Have we become so wrapped up in our technologies and possessions that we are failing to recognise the beautiful souls that live amongst us. We need to start taking responsibility and waking up to what is going on around us. In truth, we need to become more like the animals.

CHAPTER 8   PSYCHIC ABILITIES

Psychic power is the ability to download information Directly from the Universe.

Every single one of us has some degree of psychic ability. I believe that we all have sixth sense ability and intuition. The only reason it is more evident in some people than others, is that they are more aware of it, believe in it and practise it. In our logical brained society, we are brought up to think that such abilities don't really exist, and so these talents are suppressed; they are not acknowledged. This is such a shame, because these senses can make our lives a whole lot easier. Like untrained muscles, they just need a bit of a workout. And with practise, they build up and become more and more evident.

I am one of the lucky ones. I was brought up to be very open minded about such things, and so even before stepping on to my spiritual path, I had encountered quite a few psychic happenings. Your psychic abilities definitely become stronger when you start adopting spiritual principles, and my powers of intuition are now much stronger, making it easier to make decisions. I have learned to really trust that gut instinct!

I think that psychic abilities are much more recognised than we are led to believe. There are quite a few people coming forward now that describe themselves as psychic detectives. They are using their mediumistic skills to connect with spirits, and help to solve crimes. And based on recent newspaper articles, they are very successful at it too. More and more police forces are using their help and assistance. Clearly they must be successful at it, or they wouldn't be used again.

Remote viewing has been used against the enemy in war. This psychic ability allows one to perceive objects, events and people from a distance, using extra-sensory perception (ESP). Using this psychic skill, things can be viewed, by tuning into them, even from thousands of miles away. Distance is no barrier at all. During the 1991 Gulf war, the members of the US Star Gate unit used controlled remote viewing to effectively spy on Saddam Hussein's weaponry. Only a handful of people within the highest levels of government knew of its existence. The American public was not allowed to even know it existed.

Governments have also been known to use the skills of top psychics, Uri Geller being one of the most famous. The BBC produced a fascinating documentary about Uri in 2013, in which it was claimed that he worked for the CIA and acted as a psychic spy.

What else is being kept from us? In truth, I imagine quite a lot. There is almost certainly a cover-up on alien life forms. I have seen quite a few videos of people coming forward to confirm the existence of alien life.

There are a lot of psychic abilities out there, and this chapter is not intended to be an exhaustive list. I will just concentrate on the ones that I am personally familiar with.

Telepathy

This is the ability to read someone else's mind. There is not a lot of information out there on telepathy, but as a teenager I learned that this was a natural ability, and with practise, the ability could be strengthened.

My dad was a university lecturer in statistics. At one point, there were studies being carried out on the telepathic abilities of twins and looking at the statistical probabilities of them picking up the same thing. My dad decided to use one of the tests on us – my mum, sister and me. There were five shapes; a circle, cross, square, wavy lines and a star. It quickly became evident that my sister and I kept picking the same shapes. So from then on, my sister and I became really interested in it, and would keep practising. Every day, we would test ourselves. And then we took it a stage further; we would state how clearly we knew the answer. The results proved to us that we did have a telepathic link. We never achieved less than 6 out of 10, and we always got the first three answers right, which suggested to us that the ability to concentrate was key. And we were always right when we stated that we could clearly see the answer. Things came to a head one day, when we went to my cousins' house. They were eager to test our ability, so one cousin took my sister in one room, and gave her an alphabet letter to pass to me, while I was sitting in another room with my other cousin. Out of a possible 26 letters, I picked the right one. We then swapped over, and my sister had to read the letter my cousin had picked, and which I was sending her a picture. She picked the right one. At this point, my cousins freaked, and started running around the house screaming. But they weren't the only ones to have a meltdown. My sister did too. She reckoned we were getting too good at it, and the last thing she wanted was me reading her mind, and not being able to have any private thoughts. So, that was the end of that. No more telepathy.

Interestingly, we both later went on to test it out with friends, and found that there were certain people we could do it with. I had a friend, who could not only pick up on the shape, but also the colour I was seeing it in. So for example with the circle, I was thinking of Terry's chocolate orange, and she was able to pick up on the circle and the colour orange.

I had a very strong telepathic link with the last horse I owned. I discuss this in the chapter on Animal Wisdom, so I won't go into the details here. It did prove to me that this ability is not just limited to humans. I suspect it is probably more prevalent in the animal kingdom.

Scientists do seem to be more accepting of this ability. There have been a few experiments set up recently that were highly successful, displaying 90 – 95% accuracy. I just don't get why it has taken this long to be fully accepted.

Intuition and sixth sense

I have had a lot of experiences which involved intuition, so I have concentrated on the two which stand out for me.

The one occurred when I was in my twenties and still living with my parents. I woke up one night at 2.00am in the morning. Nothing unusual about that; but what was unusual, was I felt paralysed with fear, to the point I could barely move. In my mind, I had a very strong impression of burglars coming up the stairs. This feeling must have lasted about ten minutes. I managed to calm myself, and went back to sleep. In the morning, I told my parents about it. The surprise came later in the afternoon. It transpired that a house a few doors away had been burgled. The owners had been out, but when they had returned to the house after their night out, they disturbed the burglars, who fled. And the time? Yes, you've guessed it; 2.00am.

A couple of years ago, I bumped into a lady I hadn't seen for a few years. Her daughter, who has Down's syndrome, loves horse-riding. I stopped to chat; but not for long, as I was in a rush to get somewhere and I was racing against the clock. Three weeks later, I went to a neighbouring town with my son to buy him some trainers. As I parked the car, the lady I had bumped into a few weeks earlier came into my mind. I pictured us going into the sports shop, and seeing her in there with her daughter. I would then ask her daughter, if she wanted to come over to the yard to have a ride on my daughter's pony. Well, it all happened exactly as I pictured it. I was in shock when I saw her in the shop. And the girl came over a couple of weeks later, and rode my daughter's pony.

Premonition

I have had premonitions, and I have also witnessed other people's premonitions.

About twenty-five years ago, I was at work when I suddenly knew that something awful was going to happen to my horse, Tiffany. I told everyone I worked with of my fears, and spent all day worrying. As soon as I arrived home I told my parents that tea could wait. I needed to get up the yard right away because my horse needed me. When I arrived there, I found my horse standing in the field, holding up her leg; her foot was pumping blood. It turned out that she had trodden on something (we never found out what), which had taken away half her foot. She was a millimetre away from being lame for life. Luckily, there was a PDSA lady who kept her horse on the yard. She was able to bandage her up, and stop the bleeding. My horse went on to make a full recovery. But this I do know; if I had delayed getting to her, she would have bled to death. Thank God for the premonition! This is a really good example of a premonition, because so many people were witness to it.

Thirty years ago, I was working in a department with three others. One of the men went on holiday for two weeks. About half way through his holiday, one of the women I worked with had a really vivid dream. In that dream, the man had come back from his holidays. He walked in and immediately announced he was leaving and had handed his notice in. The day the man was due to come back into the office, we all waited with baited breath. Would the dream come true? Yes, but with one slight difference. As he walked through the door and announced he had something to tell us, we all chorused "Yes we know. You are leaving." The look of shock on his face was hilarious. He just couldn't believe how we possibly knew, as he had given absolutely no indication of his intention to leave.

Out of body experience

I don't know whether this next story could be classed as an out of body experience, or a leap forward in time. Whatever it was, it made a huge impression on me as being decidedly weird.

I was riding a friend's horse in the ménage. He was being a bit lazy. My friend had advised me to just tap him with the whip behind my leg, if he was ever like this, so this was what I attempted to do. Just then, one of the women on the yard came down to watch me. I was riding across the middle of the school, when I made the tap with the whip. The next thing I knew, I was sitting half way up this horse's neck, with no idea of how I had got there. Feeling totally confused, I looked at the woman watching me, and asked what on earth had happened. She confirmed he had bucked three times; a small buck, a bigger buck and then a huge buck. But I had completely missed it. Where on earth had I been? I was completely gobsmacked. Normally, I can feel if a horse is going to buck, and believe you me, it is not the best of experiences. It always leaves you quite shaken. But having completely missed it, I was able to retain my full confidence.

Claircognizance

This is the ability to just know something. I can still recall a moment thirty years ago, when that knowingness just hit me like a brick. I was standing waiting for the train, when I suddenly just knew that I was going to go out with this lad from work. I must emphasize here, that at this particular moment in time, I had no designs on him at all, so it certainly wasn't wishful thinking. At this point, we were nothing other than friendly towards each other, and there was no reason to think that anything would develop other than friendship. But not only did I know that we would go out together, I also knew that it would last a few years, but we would never live together or marry. Well it happened exactly as I had envisaged. We went out together for 5 ½ years, but never married or lived together. It was like I was just being downloaded with some information from the future. At the time, it seemed very odd, and I certainly wasn't aware of anything like this happening before. When it actually transpired, it seemed even odder. I have since learned that this is an actual psychic ability.

Clairsentience

This is the ability to feel something, like a rapid change in temperature, or to feel energy. Since I have been Reiki attuned, I am far more sensitive to the feeling of energy around me. I will sometimes feel a very intense tingling around me, which is supposedly indicative of an angel or spirit presence.

When I lived at my parents' house, I often had the feeling when I awoke, that someone was sitting on the end of the bed. I would feel them get up from the bed and walk towards the door. This would cause me to open my eyes, to try and see them before they reached the door. There would be no one there. When this happened I would always feel very strong maternal love around me, so I always felt it was perhaps my grandmother keeping an eye on me. It was comforting and didn't worry me.

What did worry me was something that happened a couple of times; again, while I was in my twenties and living at my parent's house. I would wake up, and feel someone lying next to me. I would be able to feel their weight in the bed, the warmth of their body next to mine and hear their breathing. Absolutely terrified, I would open my eyes, to find no-one there. This experience was deeply unsettling; made worse by the fact that I was reading a book at the time which a friend had bought me, which described a situation exactly like mine. I read this, just days after it had happened to me. The author claimed it was this experience that forced him to recognise he was psychic. For a couple of nights, I was terrified to go to sleep. Luckily, I never had this experience again, but this may have been due to the fact that I prayed for any psychic ability I had to be closed down. I just wanted to be normal. And my prayer was answered, because from that moment on, until I prayed to be able to talk to animals, about twenty years later, I don't think I had a single psychic experience.

Clairolfaction

This is the psychic ability of smell. Just two weeks before Tiffany died, I walked out of the bathroom having washed my hair, and was suddenly hit by a very strong smell. This surprised me, because my sense of smell is very poor, and strong smells are something I don't usually have to contend with. The smell stayed with me for about 2 hours. The rest of the family claimed not to be able to smell anything. I just dismissed it in the end as one of those things.

Two days after Tiffany died, we were at the symphony Hall in Birmingham, to watch my daughter, Lauren's orchestral performance. As we sat having a drink, the smell suddenly hit me again. Again, no one could smell anything. This time, it struck me as odd. It was so strong, and it was the same smell as before. This time it lasted until I went to bed, but it had gone when I awoke.

Over the years, this happened frequently and randomly and it was always the same smell. It would appear literally within a second. Sometimes, it would only last minutes; other times, hours. It would then disappear as quickly as it had appeared.

Because smell has always played so little part in my life, I was at a loss to describe it. That is, until we had a demonstration at the yard, of aromatherapy oils. As soon as I put my nose over the bottle to smell them, I was able to recognise the smell as being the same as the ghost smell. At last I was able to identify it.

I know that when a departed loved one dies, it is possible to smell their perfume or scent around you, and this is a sign that they are not far away. I know a few people this has happened to. But I could not think of anybody I knew who had died, that were into aromatherapy oils. I do have a Native American spirit Guide, and I have since discovered that they worked with aromatherapy oils, so I do wonder whether it his presence that I am picking up on. I don't suppose I am ever going to find the answer to this one!

Clairaudience

This is the ability to hear something psychically. I actually think this one is quite common, as I know a lot of people who experience it.

Most often, it happens the moment you wake. In my case, I hear my name being called, or I might hear a strange ringing noise, the sound of a gong, or words being spoken. The moment you open your eyes, it disappears. For me, it feels like I am tuning in to the invisible realms.

Sometimes, the voice calling us can be helping in some way. Recently, my husband had gone to work, but I had fallen back to sleep. I suddenly heard my name being called very loudly, but it was my husband's voice. I shot up and looked at the clock. It was 7.30am. My husband had gone to work 30 minutes before, so it was not him calling me. I took it to be the angels – as they can mimic voices- and I felt very grateful to them. It was a work day, and if I had slept in any longer, I would have been late for work.

I have read many accounts of people's lives being saved by a voice shouting instructions at them; usually departed loved ones. I also know someone who fell asleep at the wheel of her car, only to be awakened by a voice shouting at her to wake up. It saved her life.

Clairvoyance

This is the ability to see things outside the normal realm.

I sometimes have visions of things when I wake in the morning, and before I open my eyes. One of the most significant was of the two dolphins rearing out the water (see chapter 7 on animal wisdom) and this carried a lot of meaning for me. Another time, I could see a tunnel of light in front of me. I was venturing towards it, but chose to veer off to the side and not go down it. Although intrigued, I was also scared that I may not come back.

I do have a few friends that are able to see spirits, but this is something I have never personally experienced. Again, this is a clairvoyant gift.

What is very evident in the above accounts is that a lot can be picked up in that moment between being fully awake and asleep. They do say that it is at this time that we are at our most psychically aware, since we are in a state of awareness that can tune into the invisible realms.

I think any psychic talent can be practised and improved. If you are keen to do this, there are many books on the market that will help you. As with any ability, the more you practise, the better you will become. It is to be recommended, as the skills can really help you in life.
And after all, we might as well make use of our full range of talents and abilities.

CHAPTER 9   SIGNS AND SYNCHRONICITIES

If you take a single step toward positive change, that divine energy will take a hundred steps toward you. New worlds and unbelievable possibilities will open up for you. The synchronicities that will begin appearing in your life will become a source of delight and amazement.

Joan Z. Borysenko

Now that I am more spiritually aware, I am amazed at the signs and synchronicities in our lives. I can't believe that I once thought that everything was random and coincidental. Heaven is talking to us all the time and we just need to learn to take notice. When we do, life becomes much easier, because the signs can help us to navigate our way through life's path, and we can come to a deeper understanding. As your soul path becomes clearer, and you start living a more authentic life, the signs and synchronicities become more and more common. I am at a stage now, where every day I feel like I am conversing with the Universe - when I ask for guidance or answers to my questions, the signs come in thick and fast. It is a great feeling to feel so supported and guided.

There are so many ways that heaven can talk to us. If we notice, and we see it as a sign from heaven, then it almost certainly is. And certain signs can start to appear quite prominently. As detailed in the first chapter, the sunflower was an instrumental sign for me that my horse was residing in a beautiful and joyful place. But since then, the sunflower has become a clear sign from the Universe to let me know when something is right for me. So if I pick a book up with a view to buying it, and it opens to the picture of a sunflower, I know it is the one for me. This recognition has also helped me pick our holiday cottages. Since Tiffany's death we have stayed in some beautiful holiday cottages in Wales. And here is the strange thing! All my favourite cottages, in their fairytale settings, with their large mature gardens, suffused with healing energy, have all had one thing in common. They have all had a picture of a single sunflower inside the cottage. For me, this has felt like the Universe is giving them a stamp of approval. This proved particularly helpful when picking a holiday cottage this year. I had left it a bit late and was struggling to find a cottage that was in the right location, and which ticked all our boxes. That is until I came across a cottage that had a picture of a single sunflower in the bedroom. As soon as I saw this, I knew it was going to be the perfect cottage for us. Sure enough, it ticked all our boxes, so I booked it up. And yes, it was ideal. I feel so healed and rejuvenated after having spent a week in that wonderful cottage, with its beautiful garden. So you see, once you recognise the signs and their meanings, it can provide you with very useful guidance indeed.

Signs after death

The most common time that people notice heavenly signs is following the death of a loved one. The events which followed the death of my horse, was the first indication that heaven was communicating with me. I was in such a state of awe that I was telling everyone about it. Now that I am older, I have lost my self- consciousness, and no longer worry about what other people think. I would much rather tell the truth than keep it to myself. I feel it is very important to get our stories out there, as it is the only way we can learn the truth of our existence. I intuitively know the people I can tell my story to. Unusually for me, as I started writing this book, I told it to a complete stranger. We were on holiday, and walking up from the beach. I got chatting to a woman with a couple of dogs, and within minutes of meeting, I was giving her the full version of events. The story fascinated her, because surprise, surprise, she was very spiritual and owned a couple of horses. I had known neither of these facts before recounting my story to her. She also gave the impression that she was having a bad day, and this had cheered her up no end. I have no doubt whatsoever that the universe put us on the same path that day, and for whatever reason, she needed to hear that story.

About half the people to whom I related my awakening story returned the favour. Particularly common, were stories involving feathers or butterflies. I talk more about butterflies in the chapter on animal wisdom. But the dead also communicate in more unusual ways too.While proof reading my book a friend asked if she could include something that happened to her. This is her story in her own words:-

It was a beautiful Saturday morning and I was walking around my garden. The time was about 10am. Suddenly a buzzing noise drew my attention to a damson tree. When I looked more closely, there was a large, round, moving mass of bees, swarming around a hive, which was hanging from one of the branches. Horrified and not knowing how to get rid of them, I decided to phone a beekeeper and get some advice. He simply told me to leave them alone, as they would be gone in a day or two. He informed me that the bees were swarming around the Queen Bee to protect her. At 12 noon the phone rang. It was my cousin, ringing to tell me that her mum (my aunt) had died unexpectedly in her sleep during the night and she had been found dead that morning. As I reeled from shock, a revelation suddenly dawned on me. My Aunt's nickname was Queen Bee. I knew this synchronicity was no coincidence and my Aunt was sending us a message that she was protected and in a good place. It was a huge comfort to have had this amazing sign. The next morning, the hive had gone.

This story just proves that signs from our loved ones can appear in the most unusual ways. We just need to be vigilant and be aware that if we recognise it as a sign then it most certainly is.

Another of my friends also has an incredible story to recount. Like my experience with the sunflower, it is proof that the world around us isn't so physical as we like to think. But what is also particularly wonderful about this story, is it offers proof that those who have transitioned still retain their sense of humour when they pass to the other side. This is the story told in my friend's own words:-

My husband's grandfather had spent the last few weeks in a respite home, before passing away. Just before he went into the respite home, he had purchased a bed, which had never been opened. On his death, my husband rang the bed company, to see if they would have the bed back and refund the money. They agreed to do this on the condition my husband delivered the bed to them. So my husband borrowed an open top truck, and with his father's help, they loaded the bed onto the vehicle. Having strapped it securely inside, they stood by the truck, and had a little chuckle, reminiscing about granddad and what his reaction would have been to having his bed paraded through the street. He had always been a very private man and would not have been amused by the fact that his bed was there on full view to all and sundry. My husband took a photo of his dad standing by the bed on the truck. But granddad was to have the last laugh. For when they returned home and downloaded the photo on to the computer, there was no bed to be seen; just my father-in-law standing by an empty truck. The photo was enlarged and printed off and the story was related at his funeral.

My friend has never tired of telling me this story, which occurred about ten years ago, and I love hearing it. That is one funeral where everyone attending must have felt really cheered and uplifted!

Dreams

Dreams are a particularly common vessel for passing information to us. Our subconscious can send us messages by the use of metaphors and symbols in dreams, although most of us struggle to interpret the meaning. Through practise, it does become easier to decipher dreams. At the moment I keep dreaming about a baby who is very advanced intellectually for his age. In my dreams, he is about six months old, and talks in sentences. I have taken this to mean that I should call in the wisdom of my inner child, as this will advance my progress.

Much rarer, are what I call "Dream visitations". These are dreams, which due to their vividness, and other qualities, are a connection to a departed loved one. The most significant dream visitation came to me a couple of years ago. I recorded it immediately, as it was so amazing. This is the story.

I had been a close friend of Jon in the 10 years before he died. From early on in our acquaintance, he used to tell me that he was not going to make thirty. He died when he was 29. At the time of his death, I felt anger towards him. He had killed himself because the woman who he proposed to had turned him down. He couldn't cope with the rejection. But how unfair, to burden her with such guilt!

As I became more spiritually aware, I developed more of an understanding and compassion. I recognised that in a lot of respects, Jon was just too good for this world. He was so kind and big-hearted, and he felt things so deeply. I made my peace with him.

One evening, after a bad day, I felt unusually low and disheartened. As I meditated, I asked, if during the night I could be comforted by something from the higher realms. Since entering this spiritual phase of life, unicorns and rainbows have become very significant to me, for reasons that are too long to go into here. So, I decided that I would particularly like to be sent a unicorn. I went to sleep, thinking the words, "Please send me a unicorn." Well, the long and short of it is that I received something better. The dream was far more vivid than is usual for me, and on waking at 3.00am in the morning, I could remember every detail. Jon appeared, looking happy and radiant. The love that emanated from him can only be described as heavenly love. It was so comforting and joyful, and much more intense than the love you feel on earth. I was reflecting the same love back to him, and was so delighted to see him. In the dream, I was having electrical problems, and Jon explained that he had appeared, to help me out. "Whenever you need help", he stated "I will always be here for you." Electrics sorted, he left. Later in the dream, I was clearing out a barn and brushing out cobwebs and spiders. I was hating the job and wishing I had assistance. Jon appeared again, repeating the same message as before. He sorted it for me, and left. Then I awoke with a start. I couldn't doubt the reality of the dream. Not only had it been incredibly vivid, but on awakening, I still felt the joy and love that I had experienced in the dream. Also, my ears were roaring (something that happens to them when I am having spiritual experiences) to the extent that my eyes were actually watering.

But the story doesn't end there. About a week later, on visiting my parents, my mum informed me that she had been having a sort out, and had found some things I had been gifted over the years. Everything she produced I could remember being given, except for one thing; a sculpture of a mother and baby unicorn, with a rainbow coloured crystal ball at their feet. I stared at it in disbelief - my two favourite things at the moment; a unicorn and rainbow. But however thoroughly I searched my memory, I could not remember ever having laid eyes on it before, let alone knowing where it had come from. It was like I was seeing it for the first time. I looked at mum blankly, but she just looked bemused. "Can't you remember? It was your friend Jon." She assured me that it was definitely him, she could remember it clearly.

Some people may say it is just a coincidence, but for me, it goes way beyond that. I had left home, twenty years ago, so why was this being handed to me now? Why no knowledge of it, yet my mum could remember? More significantly, my interest in unicorns and rainbows had only materialised in the last year, not twenty or thirty years ago when it was gifted to me. And the night that Jon appeared, I had asked for a unicorn to be sent to me.

It may seem far-fetched, but this whole sequence of events feels very special. I not only believe that Jon appeared in my dream to comfort and reassure me, but I also believe that I received a gift from beyond the grave. He may have bought it years earlier, but circumstances have worked in such a way that it is like he gifted it to me now, not then. It now has pride of place on the cabinet next to my bed; a reminder that the Universe can help us out in the most miraculous of ways.

In fact, this gift turned out to have even greater significance. Whilst writing this book, I started to notice the role that two unicorns were playing in my life. Eventually, they were to lead me to my soul purpose. The unfolding of this story, is revealed later in the book.

Synchronicity

Synchronicity is particularly evident when we ask for help. I normally do this in a prayer, or a meditation, and they both work for me. Last year when we were on holiday, a prayer was answered in this way. Most years we attempt to climb Snowdon. Up until now, we have never made it, due to bad weather closing in, or through my crying off for various reasons. On this occasion, we weren't even considering climbing to the top. Following mild food poisoning two days before, where my body had been wracked by terrible aching, we had decided that we would only walk for about an hour.

We set off in Llanberis, the bottom part of the route consisting of a steep road. My legs were already aching and I had serious misgivings about only going a short way. In desperation, I sent out a short prayer, asking for help. Literally, about two minutes later, I spotted a woman standing right in front of me, whom I joyfully recognised as one of my close friends. Although we don't see a lot of each other, because of distance and commitments, I regard her as my soul sister. I was so amazed to see her there, with her dad and her dog, because she had undergone a back operation only months before, and she had faced considerable challenges since, not only with her back, but with her mum being very ill.

I was overjoyed to see her, and considered it to be the greatest help I could have been given. She and her dad were planning on walking to the top, so we just started walking with them. Before we knew it, we were taking in the amazing views from the top of Snowdon, and thanking our lucky stars that it was such a beautiful and clear day. "The best views out of the ten times I have climbed the mountain" remarked my friend's dad.

Not only was I amazed to be standing on top of the mountain, but I had managed it effortlessly – no puffing or aching. I had been so engaged in chatting and catching up with my friend's news, that it had completely taken my mind off the difficult climb. A form of Mindful meditation, I guess! When we were at the top, my friend admitted that she wouldn't have made it without me. Her back had been hurting the last half an hour, so I had carried her backpack. Her dad is 83, and had been struggling, so there was no way that he could have carried it for her. My friend is a spiritual person, and I loved it when she remarked that our angels had arranged our reunion that day, and brought us together, giving us both the much needed help. And in so doing, we had a truly magical day!

I have told this story to a few people, and they have remarked that it was a lucky coincidence. Before my spiritual conversion, I would have probably said the same, but now, I do view things very differently and I no longer believe in randomness or coincidences. There are just too many coincidences in this story! The speed at which help arrived, so soon after my prayer; the nature of the help – my friend was the best solution to getting me up the mountain. This particular friend, who had so much exciting news to share. Of all the people in the world, how amazing for it to be her; someone who lived 2 ½ hours away, and like me, had never climbed Snowdon before. Equally amazing, is the fact that I bumped into her, just as we started the climb up the mountain - in the same place, at the same time. This was no coincidence. I always feel so excited, joyful and grateful when synchronicities happen in this manner.

I now believe that everything in our life is linked - every coincidence, as well as things from our past, present and future. They are all linked, and nothing is random or accidental. When you are synchronized with something you truly want, then the universe will pick up and tune into that frequency. This increases your chance of making it happen. The more you believe in synchronicity, the better the chance you have of achieving your aims and dreams, as you are sending out a strong signal to the Universe. If you tell yourself it is just random and coincidental, then you are sending out a weak signal to the Universe, and it is less likely that your dreams will materialise. So, have faith and just believe.

Synchronicity can also work against you, as evidenced by Murphy's Law. I have seen this occur with a lot of people, so watch your thinking with this one! Basically, you start believing that everything is going badly for you. So guess what? You are syncing with your inner negativity and sending this frequency out into the Universe. The result being that you attract more bad luck, as you draw it to yourself like a magnet!

Now I am aware of them, I delight in the messages, signs and synchronicities that the Universe brings into my life, often on a daily basis. It makes life so much easier, to know that we are supported in this way. This is explored further in the next chapter on "Angels".

CHAPTER 10   ANGELS AND SPIRIT GUIDES

For every fear that shakes your peace,
For every night you feel alone,
For every moment you lose a little hope,
There is an angel who whispers,
"I am here"

Anna Taylor

Angels

I have never doubted the existence of angels. It is a beautiful concept and I believe that Angels are God's gift to man. Angels are different to spirit guides, as they have never lived a mortal life on earth. As a result, they are pure celestial beings of light and love. They are here to offer assistance, guidance, security and comfort. My Nan believed she was healed by an angel (see her story in chapter 2) and due to her miraculous recovery from the jaws of death, I really can't see how there is any other explanation. In short, angels offer us unconditional love and support, and try to make our lives easier. I love Lorna Byrne's and Doreen Virtue's books on angels, as they give a clear picture of the many ways that angels serve us and the world. The big thing to remember with angels is that they can't interfere with free will;

so to some extent, their support does have limitations, but not if you learn to ask for their help.

The angels' actions are always to create more love in the world. Those voices in our head, asking us to be more compassionate; more empathic; more forgiving; more loving, are those angel voices. They know that if each and every person in this world could find their true, divine self, then we could create heaven on earth. This is what they are trying to lead us to.

But angels don't just want us to be more loving. They want us to be more joyful too. It is their wish that we can open our eyes and recognise the beauty that surrounds us and discover the joy in just being; that we come to realise the precious gift of life. In Lorna Byrne's books, it is very clear that the angels have a great sense of humour and love to make us laugh. Those times when our heart sings, they are singing along, feeling our joy.

I experienced the angels' sense of humour on a Christmas shopping trip, and it did cheer me up. I had gone shopping for a couple of Christmas presents. I knew exactly what I was getting, and only needed to enter two shops. I promised that on no account was I going to treat myself to anything. I was there to buy presents, and that was all I was going to spend money on. As I was waiting to pay for my first gift in a card shop, I noticed a beautiful angel

147

bookmark, positioned right next to me on the till. I reached over, and read the moving message. The temptation to buy was so strong, but I was determined to resist. I walked out of the shop feeling a bit annoyed with myself. It was only a bookmark after all. Not a mega spend. Next, I walked into a bookshop, and as I waited to pay for a book, I noticed a beautiful angel diary. A closer examination of it, found it to be just exquisite. It took a great deal of determination to walk away from it. As I walked to my car, I started beating myself up. It is not every day that you see such beautiful angel gifts, and I would have loved both of them. Feeling frustrated, I climbed into the car and turned on the radio. The words of a song came booming out the speakers "There's a multitude of angels and they are playing with my heart." (Eurythmics). The joke was not lost on me! I roared with laughter. Angels can have a wicked sense of humour!

There are literally millions of angels here on earth. The more specific types of angels are discussed below:-

Archangels

There are seven Archangels, and they are hugely important, being responsible for the rest of the angels here on earth. The four main ones are:-

Michael

Associated with Fire, and the colour blue, he leads all of the holy angels, and often works on missions that involve fighting evil, proclaiming God's truth, and strengthening people's faith. He empowers people to let go of fear and live with the passion of being on fire with love for God. He is a great protector, and when carrying out healing or other such practices, I always ask for his protection from negative energies and entities.

Gabriel

Associated with water, he communicates God's most important announcements to humans, and specialises in helping people to understand God's messages and applying them to their lives. He also urges people to reflect on their thoughts and emotions and helps them clearly understand the messages which they think and feel. Finally, Gabriel encourages people to pursue purity to move closer to God.

Raphael

Associated with air, and the colour green, he is God's main healing angel, and he cares for the health of people, animals, and every part of God's creation. He helps people to break free of burdens, make healthy lifestyle choices, and become the people God wants them to become.

Uriel

Associated with Earth, he focuses on wisdom, often working on missions of helping people learn more about God, themselves, and others. He grounds people in God's wisdom and gives them down to earth solutions for their problems. He also acts as a stabilizing force in people's lives, helping them live at peace within themselves and in relationships with God and other people.

Guardian Angels

These are with us throughout our life, and every person, on their conception, is allocated a Guardian Angel. They see the divine in us, and try to put us on our true path. They know what our soul purpose is, so if we ask them for help, they will do everything in their power to put us on the right path. Our behaviour may cause them despair or to rejoice, but they will never ever judge us. Throughout our life, they will love us unconditionally. I find it so comforting to know that there is an angel by my side, loving me unconditionally.

Angel's love to be asked for help, and will try to give you clear signs that they are around. Feathers are a popular calling card, and for me, this is one of the most common signs that angels are around. Recently, I read that angels like to leave coins around. I said to myself, "Well that is something they don't leave for me." The very next day, whilst cleaning the dining part of the kitchen I found a £1 coin under a cupboard. No-one takes money into that part of the house, and following on from my thought the day before, I knew it was the angels who had left it. When I first started on my spiritual journey, a few times I lost my glasses (in my glass case) in my bag. I would take everything out looking for them, as would my daughter, then my husband. After a few days of them not turning up, I would meditate and ask my angels to please put them in my handbag; every time, I would open my bag to find them right there, without even having to look. By the third time, I didn't even doubt that they would be there. I believe this was the angels' way of making me aware of their presence, and teaching me that I only have to ask them and they will come to my aid. Now, when I lose things, I always ask for the angels help and they always deliver.

I can often feel an angel around me, as my whole body starts to tingle, like someone is merging with me. Other times, I have felt my head being cradled or my hair being stroked. Frequently, when reading my spiritual books or meditating, one of the lights in the bedroom starts flickering on and off. I know it is my angel letting me know she is with me.

There are a multitude of ways that angels help us, but for the most part we are oblivious. They can put ideas in our head, and I believe that the loving ideas that come to us are put there by our Guardian Angel. Sometimes, their help is on a supernatural level. One of their most unusual forms of help came when we were on holiday. We had gone to a restaurant to eat a meal, following a trip to the beach. We were sitting outside, and we had picked a table at the end of the seating area. We sat down while my husband went off to get drinks. Whilst he was gone, we decided to move tables – ours was small, and the ones in the middle were much larger. We moved and sat down. We then heard the sound of a phone ringing – and the ringtone was identical to my phone. But I knew it wasn't mine, because I had left it in the car. We looked around. There were only about three other lots of people sitting at the tables, and none were answering their phones. Strange, I thought. A few moments later a lady came over to our table carrying a bag that we had left at that first table. She explained that she had heard a phone ringing from the bag, which had alerted her that we had left it behind. I thanked her, but then became confused. Because none of us had a phone with us, so how could the ringing have come from the bag? Furthermore, that lady and her family were the only people sitting in that half of the restaurant, so it couldn't have been someone else's phone. We did check the bag just to make sure, but there was no phone inside. I truly believe that the angels had created that ringing, to make sure we didn't lose the bag. Inside it was my kindle, with all my spiritual books on, a lot relating to angels. In fact I was halfway through reading a Lorna Byrne book on angels. I would have been devastated to have lost that Kindle. And thanks to the angels, I was spared the pain.

It is possible to learn to connect to your angel, and this is very rewarding. I really recommend that you do, because the more you connect with your angel, the easier it becomes to ask for help, and to notice the angelic assistance in your life. There are lots of free meditations on the internet, which enable you to do this, so check them out. Please do not feel embarrassed to ask for help or guidance, and don't feel that any request is too large or too small. Your angel simply loves being asked for help.

Spirit Guides

Spirit Guides are different to angels in that they lived a human life. In this respect, they can be of great help, because they understand so much of the human experience, and the highs and lows of life on the physical plane. In the spirit world, they have gained a lot more knowledge, and have done a lot of training to be able to take on the role of a Spirit Guide. They reveal themselves to us when the time is right. I love the saying "When the pupil is ready, the teacher appears," because it is so true.

I discovered my first Spirit Guide after a guided meditation. I had a clear picture of him, but no name. I asked for his name to come to me on awakening after a night's sleep and immediately on awakening the name "Theostle" was in my mind. I also learned that he had lived a long time ago, and he had been a soothsayer. He has helped me a lot, and given me a lot of guidance and help when I have asked for it.

My second spirit guide came to me the night before I took my Reiki 2. He is a young Native American and he immediately told me his name was Kali. He has a strong connection with an eagle owl, Tabu, who rides on his shoulder. He is much quieter than Theostle, but he is an expert on animals and nature, so he helps me when I am doing animal communication readings.

If you are keen to connect with your own spirit guide, as with angels, there are plenty of guided meditations on the internet, which allow you to do this. Or you can still your thoughts and open your mind to receive them

Whilst writing this, I am currently attending an online "Connecting with your angels" workshop, run by Katie Oman. One of our tasks was to ask our angel for signs and messages and to keep a journal for a week, detailing all the signs that suggest angel intervention or connection. I want to conclude this chapter, by including a copy of the journal I wrote for Katie, as I want to illustrate the many ways that we receive angelic help. As the journal was written for my angel teacher, when I use the word "you" I am referring to my teacher.

SIGNS FROM THE ANGELS – A WEEKLY JOURNAL

FRIDAY – 07/10/16

Whilst muck picking the horses field, I noticed absolutely loads of feathers. Wherever I looked, there were feathers – white ones, grey and black, and a large one that was all three colours. I have never been aware of this many feathers before. The angels are making their presence felt!

SATURDAY – 08/10/16

Standing in the barn I overheard someone say "She hasn't paid me for her bedding yet." It was very loud and clear, and the only bit of the conversation I heard. I realised it was the angels reminding me that I owed money to someone for the extra bedding I had acquired a few days before. The person who made the statement was talking about someone else, but I was so grateful that I had heard them say it, because my mind had completely forgotten about the money.

Ok, so I hadn't seen the person to hand them the money, but now that I was reminded, I could leave it in their drawer. Thank you angels!

In the afternoon, I went with my parents and daughter to see the production, "Sound of Music" at the Wolverhampton Grand. It was an amazing show, and the singing was out of this world. I have never been to any show where the singing was this good. I even wondered whether the angels were joining in. It was so beautiful, that it really touched my soul on a very deep level, and I cried most of the way through. I felt very strange for the rest of the evening – like it had stirred a memory deep inside me. Interesting!

SUNDAY – 09/10/16

A friend turned up unexpectedly at the yard, arriving there just after us. She explained that she had missed her turning on the way home, and had decided to come visit us. It was lovely to see her again and to radiate in her positive, cheerful energy. She offered to take my daughter, Lauren, to a show in October half-term, which delighted Lauren. She had only been saying a couple of days before, that she fancied going to a show at half-term. Thank you angels for bringing her to the yard!

Sitting in the lounge reading, the beautiful warm sunshine sent me to sleep. As I awoke, before opening my eyes, I had a clear vision of a number 2. I remembered reading about the meaning of numbers, so I turned the computer on to see what the number 2 signified. Good news – my hopes and dreams are coming to fruition. I like the sound of that.

On the evening, we were up the yard when I bumped into a woman in the dark, fetching her horse out the field. I don't normally see her to speak to, as she is at the other end of the barn from us. I commented on the fact that she was later than usual, and she replied that she had been on a "Connecting with Angels" workshop. Wow, someone to compare notes with. I am not the only wacky person on the yard.

MONDAY – 10/10/16

The number 2 is significant again. On awakening, I recalled dreaming about a friend moving with me to another yard. The two of us moved to a yard where there were 4 ladies, but they were split into 2 distinct couples, each couple disliking the other. I walked into the house attached to the yard, and left a trail of muddy footprints across a beautiful cream carpet. I desperately tried to clean up the mess, but to no avail. The footprints remained! Whilst recalling this, I was reminded of a dream the night before last. I was in a big store, and a dog messed horribly on the beautiful red carpet. I knew it was my responsibility to clean it up, but I was distracted, and when I turned back, someone else had cleaned it up. I felt relieved they had done a perfect job, and I hadn't had to do it. How strange to dream about messed up carpets two nights running. I realised that there was a message in this for me somewhere.

Having thought about the dream all day, I just couldn't fathom it at all. So I used the meditation to connect with my Guardian Angel, to see if she could throw any light on it. She told me that the red carpet was a connection to my childhood. Yes, I could see that. As a child, we had a red carpet in our lounge and I still recall when I was 7 years old, getting up in the morning to discover our new puppy had messed all over the carpet. My mum cleaned it up. The cream carpet represents the present, as we currently have a cream carpet in our lounge. Basically, it is a reminder that I don't have to struggle with any obstacles or problems alone. As a child, I had the security of loving parents, who took responsibility for me and helped me overcome any problems I might be having. As an adult, I feel responsible for myself, and like most adults, I try to be independent and solve problems on my own. But, although my confidence has improved, I still lack faith in myself. There is no need to feel like this, my Guardian Angel tells me. The angels are there whenever I need help. I only have to ask and they will help me to make the right decisions and find the right solutions. I just need to trust and have faith – just like when I was a child.

For the first time in ages, I decided to pick a card from my Archangel Power tarot cards. I shuffled them and after a while three cards fell out together. The first two gave messages I could relate to, but the third didn't resonate with me at all. The card was the 2 of Michael and the message on the card said, "It will all be better when you make a decision." The booklet explained that the heart is in conflict with the mind, and this is making it difficult to come to a decision. Use intuition and gut feeling to choose. Although this meant nothing to me, I instinctively felt it was an important card. The 2 was prominent again – not only with the name, but it pictured 2 unicorns. Additionally, I have a very strong connection to these mythical animals. I felt that I needed to put it to one side, and to wait and see what might transpire over the next few days.

TUESDAY – 11/10/16

This was a bit of a shocker. Eating breakfast I tuned into facebook and watched your (my angel teacher) weekly card reading video, covering 10 – 17th

October. I couldn't believe it. You were using the same pack as me, and the video was taken about the same time as I picked my cards. Also, you picked three cards. As I watched your video, I wondered with mounting excitement, if any would be the same cards as mine. They weren't, but the last card you drew (The chariot), showing 2 unicorns was significant. When I checked the pack of cards, there were only 2 cards in the whole pack that depicted 2 unicorns – yours and mine. This made me sit up and really listen to what you were saying about this card. I could relate to what you were saying about pushing forward with a project, as I have recently started writing a book which I aim to self publish, so this made perfect sense. I liked the sound of it being a success – a good sign from the angels that I am on the right path. But the surprise came when you said "You have a decision to make either between heart and head or between what is right for you to do or what is not so right. A split decision to make. Go with gut, and intuition and move forward." This message is almost identical to the message on my card. So I am getting a very clear sign here from the angels that I really need to take note of this message. You mentioned in your video that the card related to next weekend. So at least I am pre-warned, and wondering what on earth this decision is about. It sounds ominous, but I am trying to think positive. After all, you did say that the decision made would be the right one, and I do seem to have the power of 2 on my side, suggesting that everything is manifesting as it should. Fingers crossed!

Wednesday – 12/10/16

Unusually for me, I woke up early enough to read some of my book. It is written by a shaman, but the chapter this morning was quite dark and a bit unsettling. What with this and the warning about making a decision at the weekend, I felt that ball of fear starting to gain momentum.

All I can say about today is that the angels came to my rescue. Big time! Whilst eating breakfast and looking at Facebook, my attention was grabbed by the picture of a single, perfect sunflower. Obviously, due to my own amazing sunflower experience, when I see a sunflower, I am always reminded of the miracles and magic around us. The sunflower now on Facebook, had a story attached to it very similar to mine. A man had been on a date, and had bought a sunflower to place on the windshield of his date's car. He then decided it was a bit over the top, so decided to take it to work and give it to someone there. On the way to work he stopped at a cafe. He noticed a woman who looked sad, and found himself being drawn to her like a magnet. He handed her the sunflower, and to his amazement she threw her arms around him and started crying. It turned out that her fiancé had died the week before, and he had always gifted her, a single sunflower. She knew this was a gift from him, beyond the grave. Not only did this gesture make a huge difference to her, but it also greatly affected the man who gave it to her. He had been in a dark place, but this incident completely opened him up to the divine and changed his life. I knew instantly the message the angels were sending me, by showing me this sunflower. "Yes, you need to be aware of the darker forces in the world, but you don't have to fear them or give them your attention. By doing so, you help them to grow. Instead connect to love and joy, and have faith in the great divine. Trust in the beautiful miracles of life and know that everything is in divine order."

Today, the angels were really drawing my attention to the beauty in nature, and rainbow colours were the order of the day. I noticed the rainbow colours in the dew on the grass, and marvelled at a beautiful display of colours spiralling out of a metal connector attached to the electric fence, when the sun caught it right. It was like watching a Catherine wheel. At this moment, I wondered why we bothered with fireworks, when we could just take children into nature and teach them how to truly see. In the afternoon, something remarkable happened, which proved the angels were listening to my request. I needed to get a bag of feed for the horses, and the shop was about ten minutes drive away. Getting in the car, I placed a cd in the player. The song "Somewhere over the rainbow" started playing. I suddenly thought how nice it would be to see a rainbow and decided to ask my angel if at all possible, could she please send me a rainbow. It had been sunny all day and now looking at the big, white, fluffy clouds in the sky, I thought "not much chance of that." Ye of little faith! I should have known better. Angels are true miracle workers. I drove out of the village, and had only gone about half a mile, when I noticed huge puddles everywhere. There had clearly been one hell of a downpour. I continued driving, and kept playing "Somewhere over the rainbow." I felt it might draw one to me. And then I noticed it. Very faint, but it was a rainbow. Wow, I just couldn't believe it. And the sky looked quite normal. I continued driving until I realised I had completely missed my turning to the shop. In fact, I should have turned a long way before I saw the rainbow. I did a detour, and about five minutes later I came over the brow of a hill. Facing me was a huge black cloud, and a beautiful, vivid rainbow. It wasn't the complete arc;

about half an arc, but it was beautiful all the same. It also hit me, that if I hadn't taken a wrong turn, I would never have seen it, because the correct route was surrounded by trees. I have to confess that I was completely overcome – and shed a few tears. At this moment, I just felt so sorry for people who don't believe in angels. They are missing out on the most incredible magic.

Thursday 13/10/2016

As God rested on the seventh day, then so did my angels. No sign of them today. But after the excitement of the last few days, it is just as well, because any more angel magic, and I would have been floating off into the clouds to join them. Today, being a work day, I needed to ground myself and come back down to earth.

Conclusion

This week has been truly amazing. I knew angels connected with us, but not on the scale that this exercise has proven. The prominent signs were the sunflower, unicorns and rainbow. These are all hugely significant to me, and have played a big part in my spiritual unfolding. I am left in no doubt that the angels were communicating loud and clear. It seems that the more of a conscious effort we make to connect, the more their signs and help become noticeable. And the more we open our hearts and minds to them, the more visible they become to us.

Carrying out this exercise seemed to open me up massively to the messages from the angelic realms. For in the weeks following, there were to be a lot more revelations and realisations, and so many pieces of the jigsaw would slot into place. The curtain was to open, and I would come face to face with my soul purpose. An unusual and profound task that I was to undertake, was about to reveal itself.

CHAPTER 11 I BELIEVE IN UNICORNS

Wherever they may have come from, and wherever they may have gone, unicorns live inside the true believer's heart. Which means as long as we can dream, there will be unicorns.

Bruce Coville

In the previous chapter I mentioned the card reading that I had carried out, and how the message and the picture of the two unicorns was so very similar to that of the card reading carried out by my Angel teacher. My teacher had mentioned that the message on the card related to the weekend and so I was getting a very clear sense that there was a decision to be made. You may be wondering what this was. Again, the clue was in the cards. My course teacher had referred to the picture on her card, as two horses, but they were actually two unicorns. And the decision as it turned out, related to my horse.

For the last couple of years, I have been working really hard on my horse's suppleness, and strengthening her weak back. And although her work is better than it has ever been, and her back stronger than ever, she had suddenly become very aggressive about having the bit put in her mouth - behaving like a snapping crocodile. She was the same when I put her saddle on and fastened her girth. Unusually, she had also started stopping and planting in the ménage, even though she has always been a horse that hates standing. And on the Saturday, as I led her down to the ménage, I heard her say very clearly "You should be using my mind, not my body. This is not what we are meant to be doing." Later in the day, I tuned into her telepathically, to see if I could glean more information. She made it very clear that she came into my life to lead me away from riding and training horses. "That is not your soul purpose. And riding is not for me either." She reminded me how easily she can tune into people's energy, and how she likes engaging with them. She also reminded me how she tried to warn us of silver's (her field mate) impending laminitis, before any symptoms were showing. Five days before he had an acute attack, she became extremely clingy and protective of him, neighing to him constantly when we tried to take her away. As soon as he was diagnosed and he was taken out of the field for his stable recuperation, she immediately went back to ignoring him again. "So what do you want to do?" I asked her. "Be a therapy horse or healer", was her reply. "Or possibly, be a mother." Ok, there were certainly some big decisions to be made here, and a lot of thinking to do. The cards were right. There was a conflict between my head and my heart. Do I listen to the logical thinking of my head, telling me this is just ridiculous – ignore it all and carry on with the riding and training. Or, do I listen to my heart, telling me that I know animal communication is for real, and I should be listening to my horse. I needed to get to the bottom of what she was trying to tell me and I needed validation of what I thought she was saying.

An opportunity arose on the following Monday night. Looking at Facebook, my angel teacher had put a message on, asking if anyone had an animal with problems. She was running a feature in a magazine, and needed people to come forward. I pondered it. Nobody else had replied, and I didn't particularly want to feature in a magazine. I decided to ask the angels, as to whether I should send Jazz's details. I picked up my pack of angel cards. If the answer was "yes" I asked for a card to fall out that depicted a horse or unicorn on it. I shuffled them, and immediately knew the answer. The card that had fallen out showed two unicorns. It was "the chariot," the card my angel teacher had picked out the week before. There couldn't have been a clearer sign. So I replied to her message and explained about Jazz's grumpiness around tack and riding. I didn't mention the messages Jazz had given me, as I wanted to keep it as open as possible.

It appeared that she had been tuning in to the animal's aura. She explained that Jazz was very special; she had a rainbow coloured aura and unicorn energy around her, which is very rare. She was in a state of spiritual awakening. She explained that as

Jazz had become older, she was more and more aware of her special qualities. She didn't want to be treated like other horses (don't I know it) and she wanted her gifts acknowledged. I knew it to be true. Not only had I picked up on it, but my Reiki teacher had said exactly the same thing about her, a few years before. So, her spiritual nature had been validated. Now I just needed to decide what route to take with her.

On Friday of that week, I made another amazing discovery. One of the women on the yard started telling me about a recurring dream she had been having for the last three weeks. Unicorns had taken her into some woods, to where there was a full length mirror. They wanted her to follow them through the mirror, as they wanted to show her something. She was too afraid to go with them, as she was scared of not being able to come back. "How many unicorns?" I asked, although I already knew the answer. "Two." Also, through the mirror she could see a waterfall and a rainbow. My special place I visit when I meditate is next to a waterfall, and it is bridged by a rainbow. These two facts confirmed for me that her dream was as much meant for me, as it was for her. For some reason that I don't really understand, I never have metaphysical dreams. So, the unicorns can't reach me through my dreams. This other woman however, is attuned to the spiritual realms, and has passed messages on to people before. So, three times in the last 10 days, two unicorns have appeared. When things appear three times, then they are really shouting at you to get your attention. It is highly significant. Clearly, this woman only needed to pass this dream on to me, because once she told me, she stopped having the dream.

Later in the day as I sat on my bed reflecting on the unfolding events, my eyes happened to glance to my bedside table. There on the table was my sculpture of the two unicorns, with the rainbow crystal ball at their feet; the gift from my departed friend (see the chapter on "signs and synchronicities" for this story). Suddenly, the magnitude of this symbolism, hit me like a bolt from the blue. Could it be that these unicorns are leading me to a really big discovery about myself, possibly relating to my soul purpose? It is certainly starting to feel like that.

Who are unicorns?

I just want to interrupt the story here, to explain a bit more about unicorns. I once believed that they were mythical creatures, but having featured so much in my spiritual journey, I have completely changed my thinking about them.

It is possible that a long time ago, unicorns did actually exist in physical form. Certainly, pictures of them have been found in cave drawings, from thousands of years ago, so it is highly probable. But just because something isn't physically present, and we can't see it, doesn't mean it is non-existent.

Authors, Diana Cooper and Doreen Virtue, are both unicorn experts, who have written books about them. They describe unicorns as seventh dimensional beings, who are part of the angelic realms. It is claimed that now enough people have raised their frequency to a sufficiently high level, they are gradually coming back, to bring enlightenment to those who are ready. Unicorns purify us, for their purpose is to trigger the innocence of the divine self; that essence we had the moment we became a divine spark.

Diana Cooper describes how unicorns look for those who radiate a light and have a vision beyond themselves. They seek people who aspire to help others and to change the world for the better, even if it just their small corner of it. They convey strength and fortitude, to help those people achieve their aims. They work with those people, on a soul level.

It was only through the unicorns appearing so frequently in my life that I sought out these books. And what I was reading about them made so much sense, and seemed to fit perfectly, with the messages and the information I was getting from them. I now believe that I may be one of those lucky people who the unicorns are working through. And there are many reasons why I perceive this to be true. To share this with you, I need to go right back to when Tiffany died, five years ago.

Unicorn Wisdom

The night before Tiffany died I dreamed that we were together, on a soul level. The depths of harmony and understanding between us, was on a level deeper than anything in the physical realms. In this dream, I was privy to a beautiful connection between human and horse. And when the horses healed me, for the ten minutes we were in that unified bubble, I was awestruck by the sheer empathy, compassion and understanding these horses were showing me. It made me realise that we have a long way to go to understand the true nature of horses. I made a promise there and then, that I would devote the rest of my life to helping these beautiful animals. How, I did not know, but it was a promise I was determined to keep. I now believe that this pure intention helped draw the unicorns to my side. And I believe they have been guiding me ever since.

Just months after losing Tiffany, I joined a spiritual development group. It met once a month over a six month period. Every month, we picked an angel oracle card from the pack of angel cards offered to us. I always picked a unicorn card, and was the only one in the group to do so. After expressing my astonishment at picking a unicorn card for the sixth

172

time, the others in the group mentioned that it was no wonder. They went on to explain that from the moment I walked through the door, they had sensed unicorn energy around me. This was the start of my awareness of unicorn energy.

Around the time I became attuned to Reiki 2, unicorns began making appearances in my meditations. They explained to me that higher vibrational energies are coming to Earth, and more and more unicorns are working through horses as a means of progressing the soul development of humans. We are on the cusp of a more enlightened age, and part of that will be a more harmonious relationship between man and nature. In fact, our very survival depends on it.

Jazz came into my life about five months after I lost Tiffany. When my Reiki teacher met her, she commented on how spiritual she was, and that she could sense unicorn energy around her. It was no coincidence that this beautiful, spiritual horse had entered my life. To help with her issues, my path took me very firmly down the spiritual, and in the process, not only was my horse transformed, but so was I. And now, a few years on, the full extent of my horse's evolution was rearing up before me, commanding that her voice be heard. What else could I do? I was a communicator after all. With so many validated experiences under my belt, I knew that the message I was receiving was authentic. But what on earth do you do with a horse that is asking to be a healer? "I am listening to you," I told her. "But there is no facility in this country I am aware of that uses horses as healers. There are places abroad, but I am not sending you there." I needed guidance from someone else, because the solution was just not coming to me.

In spiritual circles, 11/11/16 was regarded as a magical day. The numbers 11:11 are considered hugely significant and powerful. It signifies angelic presence and communication. Clearly the angels and unicorns were on full duty, because this happened to be the day that my horse revealed all her dreams and desires. It was to be a day of revelations. And following on from those revelations, my path would be illuminated.

On that magical day, my Reiki teacher appeared on the yard, to talk to my horse. Within seconds of walking into her stable, Jazz went into a deep trance, and remained that way for about 1 ½ hours (30 minutes after we had finished conversing with her). Despite everything I have witnessed and experienced, even I was shocked by what was to be revealed. For I had never heard anything like it before! Jazz expressed her desire to form a healing partnership with myself. But before this, she wanted to co-write a book with me; a book that will give a voice to the horse; a book that will show things from a horse's perspective. As I reeled from this revelation, my Reiki teacher gave me an exercise to carry out when I arrived home. She asked me to meditate and to visualise myself in a forest. Whilst walking along, I see a full length mirror. I am to look into the mirror and see the reflection mirrored back. This is how Jazz sees me. I did as she asked. And as I looked into that mirror, I couldn't believe what was staring right back at me. A beautiful white unicorn! The shock of seeing this unicorn, seemed to kick start my brain into some sort of activity. For suddenly, I understood everything!

My soul purpose revealed

The two unicorns that have appeared so regularly; through the cards, statue and dreams, represent myself and Jazz. We each have a unicorn working through us. And their work is not only to accelerate our spiritual journeys, but also to help create a more meaningful and harmonious relationship between man and horse. In our own small way, and in our own small corner of the world, we have a part to play; a part that is probably being played out amongst thousands of others, all over the world. But even the smallest of parts can make a difference.

When I told my daughter Lauren, about Jazz wanting to write a book, she was standing outside Jazz's stable. "That is absolutely crazy" she stated matter-of-factly. The next moment, her face had turned to shock and disbelief. The words had no sooner popped out of her mouth, than Jazz glared at her, pinned her ears back flat against her head, shaking her head up and down, as if to say "How dare you mock me." That was telling her! Probably best that people keep their opinions to themselves. Jazz kept doing this, until eventually Lauren apologised to her; at which point she stopped.

The next day, I couldn't wait to start the book. My Reiki teacher had instructed me that the words would just flow through my head, and soon it would become automatic writing. I wouldn't even have to be thinking consciously. It would just write itself. With great anticipation, I moved a stool into Jazz's stable and sat there with an A4 book and pen. Jazz was relaxed, and unusually didn't even react when her stable mate, Silver, went on a ride. I meditated, called on Jazz, the unicorns and angels for help in assisting us, and put my pen on the paper. I found myself listening to a voice in my head, and before I knew it, I had written a few pages, without a single pause and without my pen leaving the paper. Wow, this was for real! We really could do this. I was so excited. Magic doesn't even begin to describe it.

Two weeks later, my deeply sceptical daughter, announced her conversion to the cause. She declared that she now believed 100%. I had written about 30 pages by then and every session had been the same. I would just put my pen on the page, and it would just write itself; no pause, and no having to think what I was going to write. It just came to me. But the biggest change was in Jazz herself. Now that she had been heard and had been given a voice, all traces of grumpiness had just vanished. I had explained to her that she still needed to be exercised, as it was good for her to be kept fit and supple. But even though there was no change in her work routine, she was without doubt, a totally different horse. Once again, this just proves that listening to our horses and considering their needs, can create a deep shift in our relationship with them.

But the unicorns hadn't finished with me yet. They had another lesson for me.

The child's wisdom

As I arrived at my six year old niece's house on Boxing Day, I was greeted at the door by my niece, wearing a beautiful rainbow coloured t-shirt, featuring a unicorn, and with the words "I believe in unicorns" emblazoned across it. "Do they do one of these in my size?" I asked her, as she whisked me off to her bedroom, to show me all the unicorn presents she had received for Christmas. The next couple of hours passed blissfully, as my hugely expressive and imaginative niece shared her love of unicorns, and confided some of her unicorn and angel dreams to me.

Later, on reflection, I did feel a poignant sadness. My niece's love of the metaphysical has certainly not arisen from her upbringing. Her parents are not in the least bit spiritual, and I have always kept my spiritual leanings to myself. So she certainly hadn't been led in this direction. It is just completely natural for her. It highlighted for me, how, as we grow, we lose our creativity and imagination; and worse, our connection with the divine and the magical. Our logical mind starts to take precedent, and as we age, the lower vibrations of Earth affect us and we lose sight of heaven. We forget, entering a state of sleep-walking through life. All the magic is sucked out of us, by a society that has become obsessed with logical thinking, forgetting it has a heart and soul.

As I listened to my niece's excited chatter about her beloved unicorns, I realised the value and wisdom of childhood. I never appreciated it as much as I did now. It also brought to mind my current recurring dream – "the intelligent baby." I keep dreaming about a young baby, about three or four months old, who talks more like a ten year old. I knew this was a reminder, to connect to the wisdom of the inner child; for it is they who know the truth. And now the unicorns were giving me the same message. "Connect to the innocence, purity and wisdom of the child mind, for that is where the truth lies."

I am a unicorn

I believed that I had put this chapter to bed. But then, another interesting interpretation of unicorn meaning revealed itself.

On a Sunday in late January, the lady who had dreamed about the unicorns, kindly presented me with a gift. She had bought one for each of us. It was a mug inscribed with the words "Unicorns are awesome. I am awesome. I am a unicorn."

The Universe likes to make its point by repeating the same message in close succession. The very next day, I was reading a spiritual magazine, when I noticed a letter a reader had sent in. She was describing a dream of being in a forest and seeing a beautiful white unicorn. The man, George Lizos, who was interpreting her dream, stated that he believed that unicorns are spiritual extensions of our souls. Being an extension of our soul, our unicorn guide is always with us, but you can only feel its presence if you tune into your soul. When you do, the balance and authenticity it represents becomes yours. This helps you discover your life purpose and helps you receive clear guidance on following and fulfilling it. George encourages you to work with your unicorn. Eventually there will come a time when you are no longer working with your unicorn. You are being your unicorn.

After thinking about it, I decide that I like this idea and again it does fit in with my experience of the unicorn leading me to my soul purpose. So the two unicorns could stand for the horse and human souls, partnering each other into a more unifying relationship. In the same way that the divine resides with us, then so does the unicorn. At our very best, we have the potential to be truly magnificent.

I finish this chapter by letting George Lizos have the last say:

The unicorn had always been real, is still real, and will always be real as a symbolic and spiritual extension of our soul: balanced in masculine and feminine energy and unapologetically authentic. Our soul had turned itself into a horned horse in an effort to grab our attention; and through stories, tapestries, songs and statues, inspire our quest to capturing it. Although we'd taken on the quest and searched for it tirelessly through the years, we'd skipped looking in the single place where it had always resided: within us.

CHAPTER 12   THE POWER OF LOVE

Darkness cannot drive out darkness;
Only light can do that.
Hate cannot drive out hate;
Only love can do that.

Martin Luther King Jr

There is something that all spiritual people agree on and it is this; love is the most powerful force in the universe and it is the only thing that can save us and bring us happiness. It is impossible to overestimate the power of love. Most people are unaware of how important it is, and how much developing a loving heart can change your life. But it doesn't just change your life; it changes everyone else's around you.

Every single thought, word and deed in life arises out of one of two things; fear or love. It is as simple as that. Unfortunately, our world at the moment is very much driven by fear. Our society is fear based, and this is very much exacerbated by the media. Now that I am conscious of this, I always try to choose love over fear, and my life has become much easier as a result. Love really is the answer to everything.

When we are born, love is our default setting. As a child, it is so easy to love the people around you. As for hate or prejudice – very young children just don't feel these things. It is completely unnatural. But a sad fact of life is that as we mature, and take on life's knocks and baggage, we naturally start to close down our heart to protect it. When your heart is fully open and loving, you become more vulnerable and it is easier to get hurt. So we build protection around it, but in truth, this does not serve us. Lorna Byrne describes this beautifully in her angel books. The angels show her how people's hearts are closed off. She finds it quite heartbreaking to witness. For when we close down our heart, we lose touch with our divine self, and we lose our connection to God, nature and other people. In other words, we choose separation over connection, and in so doing we cut ourselves off from universal love. It becomes a slow death, similar to a flower being cut off from light and water.

Divine Love

I have been very fortunate, as on the rare occasion I have actually experienced divine love in my dreams. Unless you have experienced it, it is very hard to express how incredibly powerful this love is. It is like nothing you have ever felt on earth. It seeps through every cell of your being and you feel incredibly comforted, knowing that you are loved so unconditionally. When I met my deceased friend in a dream – I knew it was a visitation, just by the divine love that was flowing between us. It was so incredibly intense and beautiful. I have described this experience in the chapter on signs and synchronicities, so I won't repeat it here. Another very memorable dream, where divine love was flowing through me to a young girl is described below:-

In the dream, I had been to a pop concert with my daughter and her friend. We were in a large room, surrounded by young girls, all queuing up to sleep with the young lads in the pop group. It was quite seedy – there was an adjoining room with four or five beds in, and each lad was lying in a bed, waiting for these girls to be brought to them. I was standing in the middle of the room where the girls were queuing up, and I was paralysed with horror. I literally could not move. I wanted to grab my daughter and friend, and run for it, but my feet were just stuck to the floor. After a couple of minutes, I realised there was a reason for me being there, and I also knew that my daughter and friend were safe and would come to no harm. As I stood there, a young girl came out the room, crying. I called her over and asked her to come and sit with us. She only looked about 12 years old, but when I asked her age, she replied that she was 20. I knew this to be untrue, but left it at that. I suddenly felt an immense love flowing through me to this girl. I really felt her pain, and started crying in sympathy with her. I told her how beautiful she was, and she could be anything she wanted to be. She had her whole life in front of her. I warned her, "Don't let anyone treat you like a plate of meat, you are worth far more than that." I also pointed out that behaving irresponsibly like she had tonight, would eventually lead to her becoming dead inside. I pleaded with her not to let that happen. She needed to love and respect herself. As I finished talking, her face became radiant and she started to light up like an angel. She thanked me, agreed I was so right, and stated she was getting out of there immediately. At that point I awoke.

On awakening, I felt in awe of the immense love I had felt in that dream and the beautiful words I had spoken. It seemed that on some level, I had really connected with a young soul out there, and had given her the strength and wisdom to heal from a damaging situation. The other thing that struck me was this; why am I not feeling this level of love on the earthly plane, in my physical body? If we all felt this much love and compassion for each other, then we really could create heaven on earth. It feels that this intensity of love, gifted to me in this dream, is the benchmark for how we should be towards others. And that this is the level we need to attain to reach enlightenment. Looks like I'm here for a few more lifetimes yet!

I believe that love is a far more effective tool than punishment when dealing with bad behaviour. There is an African tribe, which, when someone does something they consider hurtful and wrong, they instantly recognise as a cry for help. They are taken into the centre of town, and the whole tribe surrounds them. For two days they will remind the person of every good thing they have ever done. By doing this, they are trying to reconnect them with their true nature, reminding them of who they really are, until they fully remember the truth from which they had been temporarily disconnected. "I am good." Not surprisingly, it is rare for someone to act badly, so these ceremonies are relatively infrequent. If only our society had this level of understanding and compassion. Punishing people for their misdeeds only hardens their heart and disconnects them even further from their true self. In short, they become damaged, and their behaviour worsens.

The importance of self-love

Something us humans seem to find very difficult, is to learn to love ourselves. Most of us are so self-critical. We compare ourselves to others, and feel that we just don't match up. We are not beautiful enough, or clever enough, or sporty enough, or thin enough. The list goes on. But the truth is, each and every one of us is perfect just the way we are. We are our own true self, unique and beautiful, with our own gifts and talents. And in our uniqueness, we have something to offer the world that is different; that has our own brand on it and will help others in some way.

In order to love others, you need to love yourself. When Whitney Houston sang the lines "Learning to love yourself. It is the greatest love of all," she hit the nail on the head. Not only is it the greatest love of all, but it is also the most important love. Everything depends on it. Anita Moorjani, in her book "Dying to be me", discovered in her Near Death experience that self-love was more important than anything. She realised that by putting everyone else first throughout her life, she had neglected herself, and this was one of the factors in her developing cancer. The truth is, you were born to be loved and completely lovable.

The return to love comes easiest when you connect with your true self. If you are on a spiritual path, the goal to self-love happens naturally. I can vouch for that because it has happened to me. I have included below some steps to self-love given by Deepak Chopra:-

1. *Make contact with your inner self through:-*
   Meditation
   Self-reflection
   Contemplation
   Quieting the mind for a few minutes every day.

2. *Honestly face your inner obstacles and resistance.*

Anxiety normally represents feelings from the past that can be healed. They want to be released, and will be, if you give them a chance. Just recognising the obstacles is a start.

3. *Deal with your old wounds.*
   As negative emotions are released, you will likely find that you are stuck with resentments, hurts and scars that must be dealt with. Beneath the scar, such wounds feel very fresh. It may take help from someone who understands the situation to go into these dark places, bring them up and allow them to heal.

4. *Forgive your past.*
   Self acceptance is required first, and the realisation that you and everyone around you have been doing the best they can from their own level of awareness.

5. *Accept where you are right now.*
   When you have a bad memory, say "I am not that person anymore."

6. *Form relationships where you feel loved and appreciated.*
   Spend time with people who reflect the love you see in yourself.

7. *Practice the kind of love you aspire to receive.*

Like attracts like, and the more you live your own ideal of love, the more your light will draw the same sort of light to you.

A week after finishing this chapter, I checked my emails and discovered an email sent to me by Hay House. It was an advertisement for James de Praagh's new book, aptly named "The power of love." There was a video accompaniment, in which James points out that in his role as medium, one of the most common messages that the Deceased share is that they want the living to know how to utilise the power of love while they are still living in the physical body. James sums up the power of love perfectly, when he says:-

Love knows no limits. It is the power that holds together everything. Anxiety and worry start to fade as you align yourself with loving thoughts. Decisions are made easier. Difficult events and people will not be drawn to you, because you are learning to release that magnetic energy. When you begin to consciously surround yourself with the energy of love and acceptance – which is your natural state of being – your journey in this physical dimension becomes much smoother, more purposeful and more powerful. Be empowered with love.

Finally, I want to finish this chapter with a poem, written by Alice Herz-Sommer . She was the oldest holocaust survivor and passed away on 23rd February

188

2014 at 110 years of age. Despite witnessing the worst horrors and cruelty, she never let that corrupt her loving heart. I watched a video of her and a more loving and compassionate woman it would be hard to find. She refused to let her experiences define her. Instead, she chose to see the beauty in everything and everyone and after the holocaust she went on to live a very happy and fulfilling life. Even though she had been treated so barbarically by the Nazis, she maintained her trust in the human race, and continued the rest of her life just loving people. People who knew her, described her as having an extraordinary capacity for joy and an amazing capacity for forgiveness. Inspirational, doesn't even begin to describe this incredible person, who was clearly a very evolved soul before her physical incarnation. She understood that "hatred eats the soul of the hater not the hated." This is a woman we can all learn from, for if she can find forgiveness, joy and love, then there are no excuses for the rest of us. Her poem encapsulates her beautiful soul.

Life can be beautiful

Be always optimistic
See the good in all the bad,
As to be so pessimistic
It can only make you sad,
Never hate the haters
This will only eat your soul,

Lessons are translators
To enrich and make you whole.

Look for all the beauty
Where you can't complain,
A smile that is off duty
Only helps to fuel mundane,
Be gracious and forgiving
Learn by each mistake,
Be thankful you are living
What a difference it will make.

Be always optimistic
See the good in all the bad,
Be creative, be artistic
Be whatever makes you glad,
Bury grievances with laughter
Share loving words instead,
All your dreams go after
Never fear what lies ahead.

CHAPTER 13   THE DARK SIDE

An old Cherokee told his grandson
"My son, there is a battle
Between 2 wolves inside us all.
One is evil. It is anger, jealousy, greed,
Resentment, inferiority, lies and ego.
The other is good. It is joy, peace, love,
hope, humility, kindness, empathy and truth."
The boy thought about it, and asked
"Grandfather, which wolf wins?"
The old man quietly replied,
"The one you feed."

Originally, I wasn't going to include this chapter in the book. I wanted my book to be as uplifting as possible; a formula for joy, peace and love. But, I realised that by not including it, I am not giving you the full picture. Living as we currently are, in a third dimensional reality, duality is very much part and parcel of life as it currently stands. There can't be light without dark; or love without hate. If we ever move into a higher dimensional reality, then this will no longer be true. In this state, we can hopefully banish the dark for good. But unfortunately, we are not there yet. And whilst there is darkness, people need to be aware of it; able to recognise it for what it is. For when you are conscious of it, you can do something about it.

Evil is energy that is totally devoid of light and love. Where there is evil, there is the complete absence and rejection of the divine and God. I do not understand why anyone would choose the path of darkness over light. To me it makes no sense whatsoever. And in making such a choice, you are attracting the very worst things to yourself and making your life extremely difficult and cohesive. Why would anyone choose this?

As previously discussed in the book, I believe that we are all born with the divine spark inside us. I do not believe that anyone is born evil. But as well as the divine spark, we all have egos, which are essential to us if we are to function as humans on earth. But if that ego is not brought under control, then the darker side of our nature can start to prevail. I also believe that once our thoughts start to darken, then we attract more darkness. Like a magnet, we start to draw the bad stuff to ourselves.

Each of us has a choice; we can fuel the light inside us, encouraging it to burn lighter and brighter, or we can choose to extinguish it. I don't ever believe that the light inside us is completely extinguished. So however badly someone has behaved; however much they have extinguished that light; there will always be a spark, even if it is just that. And that spark can be ignited, and it can grow. So, although a lot of people will not agree with me, I do believe that transformation is possible in absolutely anyone. For as long as the smallest sliver of light exists, there is always hope.

The darkness is not just within us, it is out there in the world. Before I became Reiki attuned, I often had very frightening dreams. When I awakened, I would be fully aware of the good and bad in the world. I recently came across a dream journal from a few years ago. One of the entries dated 31/10/2012, is quoted below:-

Sometimes I have very scary dreams, and wake up, paralysed with fear. This was one of those dreams. I feel I have faced evil in all its horror. In the dream, I was shown atrocities that one man can inflict on another. They were horrifying, and although I don't want to think these things go on, I know my mind couldn't make this stuff up. The messages in the dream were very clear. Although we are all born with the divine spirit within us, some people's personality predisposes them to becoming more easily influenced by the dark forces. But it can have a ripple effect – they influence and affect people close to them, so they are drawn into the darkness also. Evil can also be presented as a great attraction that becomes addictive and all-consuming, casting its spell over an increasing number of people, like a giant wave, sweeping more and more people up, as it increases in power and intensity. Power can be very corrupting, and evil can be present in familiar faces (powerful people in prominent positions) and familiar places. There is a real battle going on in our world between good and evil, and these dreams make me more determined than ever, to live by "love and light," casting out the dark.

The darkness in the world can be very evident where powerful positions, like Presidency's are at stake. It is claimed that a lot of powerful people in prominent positions are using these dark forces, to further their aspirations. Unfortunately, these dark forces are then felt by the rest of us, as they are filtered down from the top. When you look at the world today, you can see how much bad stuff has infiltrated our systems, poisoning the minds of our young people. One example is the use of the internet. Although it is great to have information at the touch of a button, most of us have had those nasty and vile emails that come through our systems. But very young children are having access to the internet, not just through computers, but through their phones. And children being naturally inquisitive are being forced to face depravity in all its forms. There have been some horrific reports in newspapers on the devastating effects of accessing pornography from a young age, and how badly it is affecting the minds of these children. We are all handing our children computers and phones, but in so doing we are also opening them up to an invasive evil. There is no denying the fact that our children are more at the mercy of dark forces than ever before.

Spirit attachments

The very first course I attended, I learned about spirit attachments. This was a concept I had never heard about before, so I was quite surprised at what I was hearing.

It would seem that sometimes when people die, they struggle to fully pass over. There are various reasons for this; they may not accept they are dead, or they are too attached to something in the physical plane to let go, such as material possessions, drugs or drink etc. As a spirit, they occupy a certain space. If someone comes into that space, with the same personality traits as they had while they were alive, then they may attach themselves to that particular person. The effects on that person can be detrimental. They may feel out of sorts and comment that they don't feel like themselves. They can feel drained or tired, or have thoughts and feelings that are uncharacteristic.

It is thought that having a spirit attachment can be quite common. I have even seen it claimed that up to 99% of the population could be affected. The risks to having an attachment increase if you drink very heavily, or you are a drug taker. This is because at these times, you have temporarily left your body, and so it is easier for a spirit to attach itself. The common places to pick them up are pubs and hospitals. The more nasty attachments are picked up from ancient buildings such as castles.

The logical part of my mind did want to reject this at first. After all, it sounds nothing short of crazy. But, I do wonder. Often when you hear of a person doing something really bad, such as murder, it is so common to hear witnesses talk about their eyes changing; becoming cold and manic, like something has taken them over. Also, you so often hear the murderer saying in their defence, that it was a voice in their head that was telling them to do it. Other people have absolutely no memory of having committed the crime in the first place. Most people will say this is a good defence to take. If the perpetrator claims insanity or can demonstrate mental health issues, then they have grounds for diminished responsibility, the result being a more lenient sentence. But I beg to differ. For although I never realised it at the time, I do now realise that as a child, I did have an experience of a spirit attachment. This story is recounted below.

My experience of a spirit attachment

I was only about 8 years old at the time, but the experience is seared on my memory, as it was quite frightening and very upsetting.

At the time of the experience, I was very ill with Red flu. One night, I was battling a very high temperature. In my delirious state I could see a woman in my bedroom. She was dressed in black, and conveyed a sense of evil. I believed that the only way to get rid of her was to colour her out. When my dad came to check on me, I asked him for a colouring pen. Wisely, he refused. Instead of a pen, he gave me some medicine to reduce my temperature.

I eventually overcame the illness and started to recover. It was at this point that I started to hear the voice in my head. Even at such a young age, I recognised that this voice was not mine. It was nasty and cruel, and trying to play with me. And it was forcing me to think bad thoughts about a loved family member. My dad! Tauntingly, it would ask me to wish my dad dead. "It is only a thought after all" stated the voice."It doesn't really mean anything." Eventually, in my weakened state, I gave in and let the thought cross my mind. The voice was triumphant. "Just wait for your Dad to die" it sneered nastily. I was absolutely distraught. How could I have conceded to such evil? From that moment on, I could barely stop crying. I still remember watching "Wait until your dad comes home" on the television, and crying the whole way through it. In my mind, my Dad was lost to me and I was to blame.

To start with, my parents probably just thought I was weepy as a result of my illness. But it didn't take them long to realise that things weren't right with me. I still remember talking to Dad about it, as he put me to bed. I found it very hard telling him about the voice in my head, but after a lot of cajoling on his part, I finally told him everything and held nothing back. I don't really remember what my Dad said to me. All I know is that from that moment on, everything was fine, and the voice was gone. I lost my fear and was completely comforted and consoled by my Dad's words.

It is my belief that evil can't survive in a loving place and I think that this is what happened here. The love between a father and his daughter, and the prayers shared, were enough to dissipate that spirit for good. I do wonder how I picked it up in the first place though. Someone once mentioned to me that castles are full of the more evil type of spirits, and these are often attracted to the innocence and purity of a child. So maybe I had visited a castle, brought it back with me, and in my delirious state, it was able to attach to me. Whatever happened, it is now proof to me that spirit attachments are for real.

Sadly our prisons and mental hospitals are probably full of people with quite nasty spirit attachments. But as our society is unlikely ever to recognise such phenomena, these people will not receive the help they need.

If you do ever worry you may have a spirit attachment then please seek professional help. A Reiki teacher or a Priest, are probably the best people to approach. They will be able to direct the spirit to the light, and free you from the attachment. You don't want these attachments to drag you down and stop you living the life you were meant to lead.

Spirit portals

This is something else that I hadn't really heard of until recently, but since learning about them, I have actually experienced them. Portals are openings that allow spirits to enter the physical realm. They can open up for all sorts of reasons, usually when there is someone in the house who is naturally psychic and who is starting to develop their gift. These spirits will start to make their presence felt – you may be able to see or hear them, but more typically, objects are moved.

Recently, a very close friend of mine had this happen to her. Very kindly, she has agreed to let me include her story in my book. This is her retelling of events, written in her own words:-

For a few months, I awoke to see spirits walking across my bedroom floor and disappearing through the wall into the neighbour's house. It didn't bother me to start with as I have seen spirits on a few occasions, and know that this in itself is nothing to be worried about. But then, it started to take on a more sinister turn. I had just gone to bed and had closed my eyes for no more than 15 minutes. The room suddenly became very cold. I opened my eyes to find a male spirit standing next to the bed. I jumped out the bed at record speed, facing him on the opposite side and for a few minutes we just stared at each other. He seemed very real and I was able to take in all the details of his appearance and dress. He had greying hair, an expressionless face, and was dressed very modern, in a brightly multi-coloured jumper. There was light radiating around him, which is why I was able to see him so clearly. When I switched the bedside lamp on, he disappeared. On another night, a less pleasing spirit appeared with a brown cloak around it, with the whole face bandaged up. These spirits weren't just a visual presence though and activity in the house increased. One night, returning to the house, I heard something jump off the bed and run across the landing. My dog leapt upstairs barking ferociously, me following in hot pursuit, fearing there was someone in the house who was now going to be ripped to shreds by my dog. There was no one there. If that wasn't enough, the cat's ball had started to move on its own and things were falling off the table. Without doubt there was a presence in my house and I was really starting to resent it being in my space. Fear began to take over. One night when I was lying in bed feeling nervous and worried about what was coming next, the manifestation of a large dog appeared. It was straddling me with its head facing the window. At that moment, I felt an amazing sense of protection and I am convinced it was one of my deceased Rhodesian Ridgebacks looking out for me.

Unlike the other visitations, this was really beautiful, and for a while it really strengthened me. Eventually though, with the Spirit visitations continuing, my health started to suffer. I was sleeping with the downstairs light on and for a couple of weeks my mum moved in with me. I finally called in a priest to bless the house. For a few weeks everything was calm, but then it all started up again.

My nerves were so shattered I was on the verge of putting the house up for sale. But not before trying one last thing. You persuaded me to let your Reiki teacher come around and carry out a full energetic clearance. To my horror, it was discovered that a portal had opened up across my bed. Three of the rooms contained spirits, and their presence had formed a triangulation. This had made the portal very powerful indeed. Added to this, I was also bringing spirits back to the house from the hospital where I work, and one had actually attached to me. No wonder I was experiencing so much! Luckily, your hugely talented and gifted Reiki teacher was able to resolve the problem, although she had to work most of the day to do this. The portal was closed, the spirits sent to the light, and I was given a protection prayer to recite daily. Since then, I have been really struck by the changed atmosphere in the house. The calm, gentle energy that attracted me to the house in the first place now presides, and my cat is once again happy to enter rooms upstairs which she previously avoided. It has been a harsh lesson – I now recognise

*the considerable importance of asking for protection,
before carrying out any spiritual work.*

A few years ago, I am convinced that we had a portal
open on the yard where we keep our horses.
Upturned cups were appearing on all the chairs in
the tearoom. There would be a chair in the middle of
the room, with a towel placed over the back of it.
Someone would tidy the room and put it back to
normal, only to find ten minutes later that the
upturned cups were back on the chairs. To start with,
nobody thought anything of it – we all thought it was
someone having a joke. One of the women on the
yard suffered from Obsessive Compulsive Disorder,
so was spending most of her time up there washing
the cups. But then it got beyond a joke, as it was
persistent, lasting about three weeks, continuing
even when people started to get scared . One or two
were even threatening to leave. It was happening
morning, noon and night, and by keeping a record of
the people on the yard at the time, there was no one
person there at all times. At one point, someone
took a photo of the room. My daughter, on looking
at the photo, turned white. She explained that she
could see a child's face in the window. She was able
to describe him in great detail – about ten years old
and wearing glasses. When she looked again, the
face had gone. I found this interesting, because I had
felt that it was spirit activity in the form of young
children playing "schools." The upturned cups could
represent the pupils and the chair with the towel

over it, the teacher. I had not told anyone this including my daughter, so it was significant that her sighting fitted in with my theory. About this time, someone very spiritually gifted, tuned in telepathically to the tearoom. She discovered that a portal had opened and she closed it down. Only two of us knew about this, but the activity did stop from that moment on. I believe it had opened, because there were quite a few people on the yard at the time who were either developing spiritually or were "sensitive." There were at least four people who could see spirits. Anyway, it was a relief that we managed to ride it out, without anyone leaving.

Just one last thing I want to say, on the subject of spirits. As a child, I was terrified of seeing a ghost or a spirit. But through all the spiritual work I have done, that fear has gone. Those souls, who haven't properly passed over, need someone to help them. They need love and assistance, not fear. As they carry the same personality they had when they were alive, very few are nasty or vindictive. You would be extremely unlucky to come across an evil spirit. As I point out to people, I think we have more to fear from people who are alive, than from those who are dead. I met a lovely woman recently. She told me that as a young child, she could see spirits as easily as she could see people. She was unable to tell the difference. They held no fear for her. But what did frighten her was her mother telling her that she would be burned as a witch. This fear meant she lost her gift by the time she was about eight years old. This is typical for a lot of sensitive children.

I think children see spirits easier than adults, because their vibrational energy is higher. They don't have the blocks that adults have. Only recently, a woman showed me a photograph on her phone of her friend's daughter. This girl was about 6 years old. She told her parents she was dancing with her friend. But the parents could only see their daughter. That is until they took a photograph. The form, dancing with their daughter, was enclosed in a mist, and you couldn't make out the features, but it looked like a young girl in a yellow dress, her leg trailing out behind her. It was undeniably a spirit, and one of the best photos I have seen. I felt the joy flowing between them, as I looked at the photograph. How sad that our society likes to depict spirits as scary, and features them so negatively in books and films.

Protection

If you are doing any spiritual work, it is important to ground yourself and call in protection. I ask Archangel Michael to surround me with protection and I imagine myself wrapped in a bubble of white light. I ask that any negative energies and entities be kept out the house or out of my space and I ask for that space to be filled with healing light and love.

It is important to be aware of the darker forces in our lives; only by recognising them, can we deal with them. But don't give them loads of attention, or thought, as by doing so, we give them our power. Finally, if we want to make life better for everyone and create peace on earth, then each and every one of us needs to work towards this goal. We all need to spread our light. As Edward Burke once said, "The only thing necessary for the triumph of evil, is for good men to do nothing."

I want to finish this chapter on a positive note. I recently read an article by Elizabeth Gilbert, and she makes a really interesting point. Darkness and evil, always give opportunities for heroes to rise. Harry Potter is a great example. Without Voldemont, he is a very ordinary boy. Without the terrifying challenges of darkness and evil, Harry would never have had the opportunity to find his own power, his own strength, his own leadership and his own magic.

This is just as true for your life as it was for Harry. Without the presence of darkness and evil in your life, you will never be challenged to know your own goodness and courage. Your light will burn brightest in the darkness. So, go forth and shine that light!

CHAPTER 14   LESSONS IN SUFFERING

I walked a mile with Pleasure
She chattered all the way;
But left me none the wiser
For all she had to say.

I walked a mile with Sorrow
And ne'er a word said she;
But oh, the things I learned from her
When Sorrow walked with me.

Robert Browning Hamilton

One of the most asked questions around is "Why is there so much suffering in the world?" There isn't a person on the planet who hasn't asked it at some point. It is also one of the main reasons people do not believe in a God. So many times in my life I have heard people say "If there is a God, how can he allow such suffering?"

The thing is, as with so many life questions, we approach our thinking around these topics with our limited human brain. We find it hard to step out of the human framework, and perceive it in a much wider context. There are so many different ways of approaching answers to these types of questions, but we choose to limit ourselves. My thinking used to be just as limited, but now through my spiritual lens, I find it much easier to adopt a different perception.

Through my own experiences, I have learned a valuable truth: suffering is an essential growth tool and it can be our most important spiritual teacher. Our greatest struggles offer us a prime opportunity to grow. If we were born into this world, and only experienced happiness, then wouldn't we just stagnate? We would have no incentive at all to grow and improve things for ourselves. We would have no challenges or goals. In short, we would not grow or develop as a person, and there would be no evolution. And without the bad times, how can we appreciate the good times? The experience of suffering enables us to empathise with others who go through the same thing. It teaches us empathy, compassion and kindness. Some of the greatest spiritual leaders, healers and writers, are people who experienced great suffering. Through it, they found a way to combat it, and were then able to train others in their techniques and teachings. In short, they have become inspirational teachers.

Also, when we are at our lowest and most desperate, these are the times that the most beautiful things can happen to us. These are the moments that can lead to a spiritual awakening, as happened to me with the death of my horse (see chapter 1). All the beautiful and spiritual things that occurred to my family as recounted in chapter one, arose out of suffering. Probably, because it is at these times we are at our most vulnerable, and actually call out to God for help. We let our guard down, and invite Him into our lives. And he responds, and like the loving Father he is, we are given the greatest and most fulfilling gifts of our whole life – Belief, and Truth. Also the knowledge that there is more to this reality than our limited minds had perceived.

The human element

Another thing that people choose to ignore, when asking why God allows suffering, is that it is us humans who are responsible for most of the suffering in the world. God gave us the gift of free will, so that we could choose what sort of life we wished to create for ourselves. How can it be his fault, if we have then chosen to abuse this liberty? The world has enough resources to feed, house and water everyone, but we have chosen to be greedy and grasping, and take more for ourselves than we need. This has created a world where some people are ridiculously wealthy, and others have nothing. This is compounded by the thinking that we are all separate from each other, and it is each man for himself. If only we could see that we are all connected to each other! If only we all cared enough to ensure that wealth and resources were distributed equally.

The daily stories and pictures of the horrors inflicted on the children in Syria and on refugees fleeing from war-torn countries is heart-breaking. But the blame rests firmly on our shoulders. How can we allow this to happen? How can humanity have fallen to such a low? Why are we allowing fear and hate to take such a hold? If only love could prevail. If we all allowed love into our hearts, then all this turmoil could be a thing of the past. Each and every one of us has to bear responsibility for turning things around and creating a better world for ourselves and for future generations.

Ok, you might say, but what about earthquakes, hurricanes and Tsunamis? We aren't to blame for those. And they can cause a lot of deaths and suffering. Not everything is caused by humans. Well no, but then we don't really know how much of a price we are paying for our activities on earth. We are plundering and destroying much of our natural habitat, and our habits are certainly exacerbating climate change. So we can't say for sure that we aren't responsible in some way, for the natural disasters that occur. It may just be the earth's response to the way we are treating her.

Soul's desire to evolve

I do believe that the aim of the soul is to evolve, and with this in mind, a life plan is made before coming to earth. The soul may choose a bad situation or some sort of suffering for the following reasons:-

- *To balance Karma (see the chapter on Law of Attraction and karma).*

- *To help teach us lessons that we feel we need to learn in order to evolve.*

- *To help teach lessons to those around us. We may for example, want to teach others about forgiveness, grief, kindness and compassion. It is reckoned that everyone we meet in this life has a lesson to teach us or we have a lesson to teach them.*

- *To help bring about a change in law, or to highlight a situation. This can bring a benefit to thousands of people.*

Seen in this light, planet earth is very much a school, where we come to learn our lessons. Unfortunately, we can only learn those lessons through a certain degree of suffering.

One of the worst things that can happen is to lose a child. I can't even begin to imagine the heartache! When my son was about three, I had a really vivid dream; my son was riding a horse. He jumped over a hedge and landed in the sea; his watery grave. The scene jumped forwards, and I was at his funeral. The pain was absolutely terrible, and I wondered how I would ever be able to carry on. When I awoke, I was crying, but I was so relieved and thankful that it was only a dream. I think it was a warning, and it certainly made me take heed. That day we visited Tintagel. It was a very windy day and unnerving being on an island surrounded by sea. As a result of the dream, I refused to let go of his hand. There was no way I was going to allow that dream to come true. I had only felt the pain for a short time, but my heart bleeds for people who have to wake up every day with that feeling of heartache.

I do believe though, that when a child dies, their soul has chosen to do so for any of the reasons mentioned above. To get your head around this concept, I have chosen to tell a story below. This isn't necessarily how things work, as none of us know the real truth, but it is a different way of perceiving things, and I do believe that to see the real truth of things, we need to see the bigger picture, rather than viewing it from a limited human perspective.

A soul was in heaven, sitting with God and the angels, making his life review. He had been to earth many times, and had learned many lessons. God didn't think it was necessary for him to come to earth again, because he was already very evolved and in God's eyes he had attained enlightenment. But the soul felt differently. He wanted to help mankind. His purpose for coming to earth was not to further his own education; it was to help others. So he formulated his plan. He chose his parents carefully. They were kind, compassionate people, with great inner strength. His plan was as follows: he would be born into this loving family, and for ten years of his life he would be very happy. He would carry a beautiful inner light, and everyone who met him would be cheered by his happy, joyful nature. He would spread that positivity to everyone he met. When he was ten, he would develop cancer and die. He had no need to live any longer, for he had no further lessons to learn for himself, and anyway, he had much work to do in heaven. Following his death, his parents would be heartbroken and their grief would be immense. But eventually, through tremendous suffering, they would come to terms with it. They would recognise that even though this child was only with them for ten years, he brought them incredible happiness. Not only that, but he had endured so courageously through his illness, and had only ever thought of others. He had taught them how to live, and how to die. He had been an inspiration, and they felt so honoured and grateful that he had been their son. They realised that they had been incredibly lucky to have had him in their life at all – even though it was for such a short time. And for this they were grateful. They wanted to honour their son and live by his values. He had only ever thought of others. He had taught them a valuable lesson and they wanted to put it into practise. The mother decided to train as a Grief Counsellor and to set up a group, supporting other parents who had lost children. The father, who was more of a businessman, set up a Trust for which he obtained sponsorship. It would raise money to fund the research of childhood cancers, and hopefully save thousands of lives in the process. This one boy changed the lives of a lot of people and benefitted so many through his short life and death. He achieved more than most people do in several lifetimes. He proved that you don't have to live a long life to be successful. Through suffering, so many great changes were put into place and so many people were helped.

There are echoes of a great truth in the above story. It calls to mind, Stephen Sutton, who battled his terminal illness with inspiring bravery and determination to achieve his bucket list before he died. In the process he raised thousands for charity, and everyone felt touched and encouraged by his bravery. It also brings to mind, a young boy, Harry Moseley, who selflessly thought of others while he was dying of cancer. He started making bracelets, to help other children. Following his death, his mother decided to carry on selling his bracelets and set up a Trust to raise money for cancer research. To date, the charity has raised over a million pounds. The firm I am employed with agreed to act as a sponsor and she visited our firm. I was really touched by her courage and bravery, and was left in no doubt that her son had been a very evolved soul, whose light was continuing to shine. There are so many lessons these souls can teach us.

This thinking, in no way makes it any easier if you lose a child. Even with my strong beliefs, I know that if I were to lose one of mine, I would still suffer the same heartbreak as someone who believed that death was the end. And perhaps at the end of the day, it is the way things need to be. For if we knew the absolute truth, then there may be no grief; without the grief there can be no change or progress. And there can be no opening of the heart, and feeling compassion and empathy for others. So I always feel there needs to be an element of doubt or uncertainty. We can never know for certain, as this would just hinder our progress and evolution.

Physical suffering

So, how about people who are suffering physically? Again, the same sort of thinking can apply. As I write this, the Paralympics have just ended. Those young people who take part are nothing short of inspirational. Their motivation and determination to succeed against the odds, is a lesson to us all. I am a horse rider and have ridden all my life, but I would struggle to attain a good score in a walk trot dressage test. Yet, I have just watched a rider with no legs, ride a high level dressage test. How is it even possible? It makes me ashamed to admit my own shortcomings. Clearly the limitations I impose on myself are in my head.

I once worked with a man in his twenties, who was registered blind and had attended a blind school. He confided in me that he saw his disability as a gift. He had grown up with a violent, alcoholic father and a seriously depressed mother. His brothers were always in trouble. They would throw a punch first and ask questions later. But he was saved from the same fate. The blind school he attended was a very loving, nurturing environment and he learned to love instead of hate. It was the saving of him. Also, he compensated for his lack of sight by developing his other senses. He had acute hearing and a brilliant memory.

Something I never fully appreciated was how much our emotions, fears and worries, can affect our physical health. I knew, like all people, that there was some link. We all know someone going through a lot of stress in their life, whose immune system starts to get compromised. They get more colds and flu. They develop eczema or asthma. But I now realise there is a much greater connection between our physical illnesses and emotional well-being than I had ever imagined. Anita in her book "Dying to be me" discovers in her Near Death Experience, that it was her fear of cancer that caused it. When she comes back into her body, she is cured in days, because her fear has gone and she believes in being well again.

When my daughter Lauren, was twelve, she developed eczema on her right hand. It started on her thumb and spread outwards. For two years, we tried every cream and ointment on the market, but it continued to worsen until her hand was a mass of itchy, white skin. At that time I had taken a spiritual development course, and my teacher was a transpersonal hypnotherapist. She had mentioned that she was particularly successful with children, because of their ability to visualise. They don't have the blocks, like us adults. So she carried out a session with Lauren. Although Lauren was quite shy at the time, and didn't open up to adults very easily, she had no trouble working with my teacher. Lauren described a scene – She was three years old and sitting on a beach full of people. Then the people left, and she was alone with a donkey. The donkey turned to her and stated quite profoundly, "You are not alone." Lauren actually started to cry. I was not present, while they were working through this, but later the hypnotherapist told me that at three years old, Lauren had been left somewhere that had traumatised her. She had put this trauma into her thumb, and years later the trauma had been released in the form of eczema. When she recounted this to me, I knew instantly what she was talking about. At three years old, I had taken Lauren to playgroup. I had stayed with her for the first few sessions, but on the fourth session, I was instructed to leave her. When I went to pick her up, she had sucked her right thumb so hard, that it had blistered. I was horrified! And now, eleven years later, I was horrified again. My teacher reassured me that she had carried out a healing exercise with her, and she had taught her some affirmations to work through every morning and evening. My biggest surprise came just hours later. All the white on Lauren's skin had just vanished. Two weeks later, the hand was healed – there was no sign of the eczema that had blighted it for the last couple of years. Having witnessed this incredible healing, I realise we have a long way to go to truly understand the mind/body connection. It would seem that there is still a lot to learn in the field of medicine, and even more to learn about our own powers of healing. And when we do, then hopefully a lot of physical suffering can be alleviated.

Mental suffering

Unfortunately, we seem to be in the grip of a mental dilemma; 1 in 4 people are estimated to be currently suffering from a mental condition, such as depression. It seems so ironic. We are living in an age where we have never been healthier or wealthier, and we have so much in the way of gadgets and technology at our fingertips. But happiness seems to be at an all time low. From my point of view, this just proves that material possessions do not lead to happiness. So why are we so miserable?

I think the answer lies in our psyche. Now, more than any time in history, we are divorced from nature. There has been a period of rapid technological growth, but I feel there has been a price to pay. In achieving this advancement, we have replaced the nature God with the mind God. Our brains and our minds are now considered so superior, that we have turned our back on the ancient traditions and we have lost our connection to the Earth. In a lot of societies, including Western society, heart based emotion and feelings are swept aside, to make room for the intellect. Any talk relating to the invisible realms or the universe is considered backward and positively archaic. We are clever now and have risen above such things. The problem is, this has created a huge sense of loss for a lot of people. There is a sense that something is missing; we are incomplete. Deep in our subconscious memory, we know that our life here is no accident. We came here to fulfil a purpose and to find our true self. And the fact that we are being driven away from our purpose, exacerbated by our separation from nature, is creating a lot of mental suffering for people.

As I journey through life, I come across a lot of bitter people. They blame their bitterness and sadness on events in their past; parents divorce; abusive marriage; miserable job. It is so easy to blame others for our suffering. But holding on to their past in this way, means they are holding on to their wounds and not allowing them to heal. As a result, they can't move forward with their life. This is why forgiveness is so important. By not forgiving, you are simply holding on to all that bitterness and hatred, which hurts you more than anyone. It shrivels you up inside, and closes down your heart, making it so much harder to give love, empathy and compassion to others. You can't change the events in your life, but you can change the way you think about them. And you can change your thinking, so it benefits you. Let go of your past with forgiveness in your heart and live for today. The past has gone, and the future is to come. There is only the present moment, and you want to be living this, fully present, and as joyfully and gratefully as you can. For in this frame of mind, you can attract better things towards yourself.

Fear of the unknown, causes a lot of people to stick with their life, even if they are unhappy, rather than try to change it. The famous Vietnamese Buddhist monk, Thich Nhat Hanh, once said, "People have a hard time letting go of their suffering. Out of a fear of the unknown, they prefer suffering that is familiar." This is so true for many people. Moving out of their comfort zone, is just a step too far. Most of us are very resistance to change, even when it would appear to be a change for the better. We just get stuck, afraid to move forward; like the rabbit in the road, paralysed by the headlights of a car.

Although they are in the minority, you do get some people who wear their suffering like a badge of honour. They can't wait to tell you about their latest disaster, calamity or illness. Unconsciously, they are holding on to their suffering, perhaps because they enjoy the attention it gives them. Maybe it brings them the care and attention of people who wouldn't normally bother with them. As a child, I quite enjoyed being ill. I would be allowed to stay at home rather than go to school. I would be fussed over and given brightly coloured medicines that tasted really nice. If my appetite waned, mum would make the most delicious orange sorbet; far superior to anything you could buy in the shops. Yes, this sort of suffering wasn't bad at all.

My personal lessons in suffering

I always felt that the suffering in my life was to teach me lessons, and to help me grow, even before I read about this.

My biggest handicap in my life has been my shyness. Even when I was a baby, I would scream at people if they came across to talk to me in my pram. This shyness was crippling. It stopped me doing the things I would really have loved to have done, so in a sense it was very restrictive. When I started work I learned to hide it better, but until recently, even having to talk to a stranger on the phone was very hard. I would just hate it. But even so, I do recognise the gifts in my shyness. I have always been a very good listener, and am very intuitive. Maybe because I am talking less than most people, I rely more on intuition and my feelings. I find out about people, not through conversation, but through feelings and emotions. I have always found it easy to know a person's character and personality, just by looking at them and reading their energy. I discuss this more at length, in the chapter on energy. Also, I have always been incredibly connected to animals, sharing a deep love and respect for them. Animals have brought me incredible joy in this life, as with animals I have always been able to be myself and not worry about my shyness. Perhaps that bond was made stronger because I understood non vocal language so well, and used other methods to make the connection. Finally, when you are shy, you do learn to enjoy your own company, and enjoy being in your own head, so taking that inner journey has been relatively easy.

One of the hardest times in my life, was starting work. In my first job, I struggled with the exams I was taking, and so I decided to change tack and try something similar but which had a more flexible exam taking system. Again I was thrown into the deep end. I was the only woman in an office of men, who all typified some negative qualities; the womaniser; the psychopath; the bully; the ignorer. My confidence hit an all time low, and it was only through my dad giving me a book to read that made all the difference. I can't remember the name of the book, but it was a confidence builder and very much along the lines of "I can do it. I will do it." They were tough times, but I did manage to stick it out, and in doing so, I learned to be tougher and braver. Not only that, but I met my husband. So you see, there can be a light at the end of the tunnel, even if you can't see it at the time.

As for physical suffering, my worst time was when I was pregnant. In both my pregnancies I became sick around the seven week mark. I was then physically sick every day, sometimes five times a day, up until about week 23. The nausea lasted both times, until I gave birth. Unless you have ever suffered pregnancy sickness, you can't appreciate how awful it is. You wake up in the morning trying to summon all the strength and courage you can, wondering how you are going to make it through the day. It is a real test of perseverance. The sickness was really reflected in my physical appearance. I wore a white mask, and my eyes appeared dark and sunken in my skull. I became very thin, not something most people associate with pregnancy. Two weeks after giving birth, I weighed half a stone less than before I was pregnant. I often joke how my most efficient way of losing weight is to become pregnant. Through my experience I learned a very important lesson. Health is not something to be taken for granted. To be able to wake up feeling well is an enormous bonus. I really feel for people who don't enjoy this privilege. I now really value my health and recognise the importance of keeping myself fit and well.

If you are suffering in some way, please do not hesitate to seek help. It takes a lot of courage to recognise your suffering and to admit you need help, but believe me when I say there is always a solution. Help may come from a counsellor or a friend. Just sharing your problems with someone can help. I draw a lot of strength and help from meditation and prayer. When you really open your heart and pray for help, it will come – sometimes in a guise that you weren't expecting. It may be immediate like my dad's experience – that voice in your head that comforts you and instructs you what to do. Or you may just find that a person appears in your life at the right moment who is able to help. You may even receive help in your dreams, and not even be aware of it. I have had times in my life where I have gone to sleep deeply worried or upset about something and have prayed for help. I have woken up completely refreshed and revitalised, and that worry from the night before seems completely inconsequential and trivial. My perception of it has been completely transformed; Divine healing maybe?

In the next chapter I give advice on tools that are available which help remove the blocks and difficulties you may experience, paving the way for attracting better things into your life.

CHAPTER 15   THE INNER JOURNEY

If you want to find a deeper meaning in your life, you can't find it in the opinions or beliefs that have been handed to you. You have to go to that place within yourself.

Wayne Dyer

I have been on my spiritual path for five years, and looking at myself now I am almost unrecognisable from the person I was before. Outwardly I probably appear unchanged; but inwardly I feel like a different person. Although I have always been happy and positive, I lacked confidence and had very little self belief. My shyness could be crippling, although in adulthood I did a good job of covering it up. Now, it is a different story. I have no worries about what other people think about me, and as a result, I have discarded the shyness which crippled me for so long. My confidence and self belief are soaring. Whereas I used to

talk myself out of things so easily, now I have no doubt of things that can be achieved. It is so, so true that the only limitations and the only thing holding you back, is your mind. If someone would have told me six years ago that I would be writing one book let alone two (yes, my second is underway) I would have said they were totally mad. I have learned to love myself for who I am, and in so doing I have learned to love everyone else. Having found the divine in myself, I can now see it in others and in everything I see. The world has become a truly beautiful place. Having a loving energy attracts all the loving things and situations to you. I feel so connected to the divine that I can now see the many ways that the Universe is talking to me. The signs and synchronicities in my life right now are off the scale. I feel in the flow and have never felt such joy and peace.

I have set out below the many tools that have helped me to get where I am today. As we are all unique and different, it doesn't mean to say that these are the right ones for you. But I have included them to show how much they helped me. There are hundreds of helpful tools and modalities out there, but I could write a book on them alone, so I have just concentrated on everything I used. Below, I have set out general tools which will help you, leading up to the more spiritual tools later. I believe that the spiritual path can benefit everyone, but it isn't my job to force you on this path. It has to be your choice.

Do the things that give you Joy

Ok, so this is so obvious, but it is surprising the number of people who give up on hobbies and interests as they get older. There is a disease of the modern age that is affecting us all; busyness. We are all rushing around like there is no tomorrow, with barely time to think. But this is not going to lead to joy. We need to stop what we are doing and make time for ourselves. And in that time, we need to do what we love, and connect to that joy.

From a very young age, I discovered that being out in nature and being around animals gave me incredible joy. It was also my coping mechanism. From the age of 14, I was lucky enough to own a pony, and all my spare time was spent with him at the farm. I loved it so much, that I regarded the long walk down the lane to the farm as entering my dream world. Around the horses I had extreme confidence and I could be my authentic self. No fear of being judged around them. This passion for me has been enduring.

I think it is so important for every young person to find something they are passionate about. Those passions help you cope with life's difficulties and problems. Particularly nowadays when there is so much more pressure put on children, I think it is vital that they have something to which they can escape. Where they can relax and enjoy themselves.

Doing the things you enjoy, can also be a clue as to what your soul purpose might be. When I attended my first spiritual workshop, I was so excited and hanging on to every word. I was the least experienced in the group, but it was so comforting, hearing everyone talk about angels, portals and unicorns. It was great to be around people that sounded weirder than me. I felt like I had come home to my family. It was so clear to me that this was the path I was supposed to be following, as it made so much sense, and brought me so much joy. Also, I noticed how differently I felt amongst these people. Whereas I would never talk aloud in a group, particularly amongst strangers, there was no holding me back!

So, think about the things that make your heart jump for joy. And do them.

Become mindful

It is strange that as young children we are taught so many skills; motor skills, reading, writing etc. But we are taught absolutely nothing about our mind. This powerful computer inside us is completely ignored, having free rein over all our thoughts and emotions. Yet, it has incredible power over us and can make a huge difference to our level of happiness.

I can't emphasize enough how important it is to keep your thoughts positive. Our ego wants to be in charge at every turn, and in so doing, it wants to keep us small and throw water on our ambitions and dreams. It is so easy to get into a pattern of negative thinking, but all this does is suck the joy out of life, and like a magnet, draw all the negative things and situations to us.

To combat the negative thinking, it is important to become more mindful. To do this, you need to be very conscious and aware. As soon as a negative or judgemental thought enters your head, you need to recognise it for what it is and let it go. Don't be harsh or judgemental on yourself, but tell yourself that you are not going to let the ego rule and you are going to replace the negative thought with a positive one instead. This sounds easy, but I can assure you it isn't. It takes a lot of practise. Just being mindful is enough to start with, and you can build up from there. It has taken me years to master this, and I am still not perfect, but the number of negative or judgemental thoughts are much rarer these days.

All of us have days where things go badly wrong. I had one of those days recently. My daughter was supposed to be going to a dressage competition, and was really looking forward to it, as she hasn't had the opportunity to compete for seven months. But from the moment we got up, everything went wrong. The final straw came when our transport man rang to tell us that due to the cold weather he couldn't get his vehicle started, so he wouldn't be able to take us. I tried ringing and texting a friend, who I knew was going, to see whether she would mind picking us up, but she didn't see the message until hours later. Now, I could have dealt with this disappointment in two ways. The first would be cursing and cussing; wailing that the world was against me; the effect being that I would be miserable all day and take it out on all the people around me, making their day pretty miserable as well. Or, I could take the more enlightened view; that the Universe has my back, and there is a very good reason why we weren't meant to go; perhaps it would have ended all quite horribly. I later found out from my friend who went, that the warm-up arena was very hard, so you couldn't canter and warm up properly. My daughter's pony does need a good warm-up to perform well, so it may have resulted in a very poor performance. Worse, the hard ground may have damaged his legs. We will never know, but I do know that by accepting graciously what has happened, my peace of mind and good mood is intact.

Very appropriately, as I was eating my breakfast that morning, I saw this great quote on a facebook page, and wrote it down. With our day unfolding so badly, it couldn't have come at a better time.

Ships don't sink because of the water around them. Ships sink because of the water that gets in them. Don't let what's happening around you get inside you and weigh you down.

Bad situations don't have to pull you down, and they won't unless you let them. Although it may seem impossible, you are not a slave to your mind; it only believes what you tell it. Choose another thought – one that keeps you strong, positive and determined to rise above the problems.

Remember, your thoughts can keep you prisoner, or they can set you free. The choice is yours. But they are important and can make a huge difference to your state of happiness. Not only that, but a lot of people believe that your thoughts and energy vibration at the time of death determines your experience of heaven. The more positive your thinking, the better your journey will be. So it is good to start preparing for this great state of mind right now.

Believe that anything is possible

The more open –minded you become and the more you believe in magic and miracles, then the more you will experience them. It really is that simple! There are so many quotes in the New Testament to this effect. It is so very sad that in our country we have become so logical, and this brainwashing starts from the moment we are born. In thinking this way, all the magic is being sucked out of our lives and we are leading lives that are so much greyer as a result.

So much has happened to me, particularly in the last five years. As a result I have been able to let go of my logical mind, and embrace the magic instead. But I do accept that until you have experienced your own miracles, this can be a hard thing to believe. But it only takes one impossible thing to change your thinking. Once you have witnessed the seemingly impossible, you then realise that anything is possible, and you can open your awareness sufficiently for a flood of amazing things to happen and appear. When this happens you will quickly lose interest in material possessions, and the shallow things in life. Instead you will fill yourself with much deeper joy and fulfilment. Life will have meaning!

Trust and have faith

A big lesson I have learned is that the universe does have our best interests at heart; but from a soul level, not an ego level. This is an important distinction. Just trust and have faith, and let yourself be guided as to what feels right. If it isn't right, you will experience road-blocks, and will need to re-think where you are going or what you are doing.

I have learned to trust the universe, and I can now recognise the many ways it helps me. Whenever I need advice or need to make a decision, I consult my higher self or my spirit guides. They have never let me down. Even when you look back, and think that you made a decision that wasn't quite right, look for the lesson or gift in it. If we let ourselves be guided, then there are no mistakes. Everything is happening as it is supposed to.

Nearly two years ago, I decided to embark on a new training method for my horse Jazz. I talked to my spirit guides, consulted my oracle cards, and used a pendulum, questioning whether it was the right thing to do; I was getting a resounding yes. The man who was offering the training was supposedly very holistic in his approach, and his consulting room was littered with Eckhart Tolle books. In my mind, I had pictured the lessons going swimmingly. But as with most things in life, the fantasy never matches the reality. We both found the lessons stressful and Jazz being the sensitive horse she is, would be tense and reactive. However, there were so many lessons learned from the exercise, the biggest being that things aren't always black and white; every modality has good things about it and not so good things. The important thing is to be able to take away the positive. And another thing I learned was to trust my own judgement. Just because someone has masses of experience, doesn't mean that they understand or can relate to your horse better than you can. Trust your own feelings. The lessons I learned are featured in greater depth in my next book. So, if nothing else, it has given me a lot of written material. I have no problem in recognising that this was something we both needed to go through and there were massive lessons to be learned.

Look for the gifts in life's difficulties

One of the things I am becoming increasingly aware of, is that difficulties and set-backs aren't always as they seem. Sometimes things can happen, which on the surface just seem troublesome or annoying. The ego part of us wants to cuss and complain. We come out with statements like "Why does this have to happen to me?" But are we really seeing the bigger picture? That traffic jam you were stuck in this morning, which made you late for work, may have saved your life. If it wasn't for that delay, you may have been in the path of the falling tree; or in the path of the car that hit a bit of ice, skidding on to your side of the road; or unable to stop in time when that kid dashed out into the road in front of you. For the most part, when things like this happen, we will never know if it has saved us from some awful fate or something worse than the traffic jam. But it is a possibility. So try to see the bigger picture.

My dad, while reading this, reminded me of a story he had told me once before. One winter, he had gone for a walk and fell over when he was walking down a hill, landing heavily on his shoulder. The pain kept him up all night, and on awakening he felt he should go the hospital to get it checked out. He was 70 years old at the time, so best to be on the safe side. He was supposed to work that day (he was a part time lecturer), so he rang the university to tell them that he wouldn't be in. In about ten years of part-time lecturing, it was the only time he had missed a lecture. The hospital did check him over, and luckily there was nothing wrong, other than severe bruising. As he made his way home from the hospital, it started to sleet. It was the start of severe weather. Later on in the day, the West Midlands suffered heavy blizzards. The roads were absolute chaos, and a lot of people in Birmingham, where my dad worked, either abandoned their cars or were left sleeping in them overnight. My dad recognised that he had been saved from a very uncomfortable, if not a life threatening situation. His car at the time was very old, with heating that barely worked. And my dad was not only quite elderly, but he was also diabetic. He would have been in severe difficulty if he had gone in that day. He just couldn't believe his luck. Or, rather, divine providence, because that is what he believed had saved him. There was a lot of gratitude expressed in his prayers that night!

Choose love over fear

There are two choices in life. You can choose to live a fear based life or you can choose to live from a place of love. And whatever anyone says, this is a choice. Only you control your mind, so it is your choice. Needless to say, choosing love over fear is going to help you lead a much happier and joyful life, for whatever you give out, you get back. Also, by making a conscious choice to feel love rather than fear, you can really change the energy of a situation. Even a bad situation, if enough loving energy is directed at it, has the potential to be made good.

Forgiveness

So many people are enslaved by their past relationships, unable to forgive and move on. But lack of forgiveness hurts and damages yourself far more than the person you are refusing to forgive. By holding on to the hurt and pain, you are blocking yourself from love and healing.

The past should not have any power over us. It is the mind which has the power. The best way to let go of the past, is to see it as a teacher and send love to all those who have hurt you and whom you have hurt. When we let go of the past, we can take back our power, and become responsible for our lives.

See the beauty around you

Something I have really learned to do in the last few years is to really see and appreciate the beauty in the world around me. On my phone, pictures of sunrises and sunsets far outweigh pictures of people. I am amazed by how many rainbow colours are created by the sun or light catching things just right. Recently on the internet, someone had put photographs of grains of sand magnified 200 times larger. Like snowflakes, each grain is completely unique, and they each looked like beautiful and coloured jewels. Nature is just incredible! There are internet sites dedicated to showing the beauty of nature; coloured skies;

flowers and trees; lakes and streams; the list is endless. Sometimes I am reduced to tears by the sheer beauty of it all. How can anyone look at all this and not see the divine? For me, seeing such beauty is incredibly uplifting. It is why I love being out in nature.

Spend time in nature

As well as appreciating the beauty, just spending time in nature is very healing and restorative. Some scientists are now claiming that trees do have a measured healing effect on us. But flowers and plants, with their beautiful colours and aromas, can also give us a massive pick-me-up. From an early age I just loved the countryside; walking and riding in nature was very important to me. As a sensitive child with a tendency to worry about things, I always found these worries just evaporated when I was in nature, so I always tried to spend as much time as possible in the great outdoors. I do feel concern for the youth of today. More and more children are spending time indoors, attached to their laptops, phones and playstations. In so doing, they are missing out on nature's healing medicine. Could this be adding to their greater mental instability?

Take quiet time or meditate

Horses are masters at just taking the time to chill and zone out. We need to learn from them, as doing this is extremely beneficial. When you feel yourself starting to panic or rush about, try and give yourself ten minutes to just calm yourself, breathe deeply and slowly and go to your inner sanctum.

My inner sanctum is a beautiful lakeside setting. There is a waterfall, with vibrant rainbow colours arching over it. The flowers and trees surrounding the lake, display a range of colours. It is at this place I meet my Spirit Guides. Just taking myself there is instantly calming and soothing.

Meditation is all about quieting the mind. To build up, just start with a minute and gradually extend the time. I started off just picturing an apple, concentrating on its colour and texture. Or, you could concentrate on your breathing. If thoughts arise, you acknowledge them and let them go. Over time, it becomes easier to concentrate. When you are in this state, it is much easier to access your higher self; that divine part of yourself that contains the loving wisdom. This is a good place in which to make decisions from or ask questions. You will be surprised by the answers, and over time you will learn that the information is definitely coming from something outside yourself. I believe that entering this state helps us to access the universal wisdom.

The power of the breath

Breathing is just something we take for granted. It is vital for life, but the way we breathe can make a huge difference to our psychological state. When we breathe deeper, using our abdominal muscles, we are able to get more oxygen around our body. This can have a huge effect, not least that it makes us much calmer and can help us relax and sleep easier.

When we are tense and fearful, we start taking shorter breaths. This is really bad for us, and can lead to people having full blown panic attacks or fainting. It is important to recognise what is happening, and to start deep breathing. This will instantly have a calming effect.

All spiritual work encourages you to adopt deep breathing before you start. You are encouraged to breathe in through the nose and out through the mouth. This allows you to relax and centre yourself, and it also puts you in a light trance; a state which makes connecting to the invisible realms a lot easier.

Daily affirmations

Self-affirmations are positive statements that can condition the subconscious mind to help you develop a more positive perception of yourself. They can help you change harmful behaviours or accomplish goals and they can help undo negative thinking; those things we tell ourselves or which others tell us that contribute to a negative self-perception. The more you affirm something, the more firmly your mind will accept it.

For example, every morning when you get up you could tell yourself "I am loving and lovable, I am happy, I am healthy." It helps to say it three times (as three is very powerful in spiritual terms) and also to say it as you view yourself in the mirror – this amplifies the power. Repeat the exercise at night, before going to bed.

They reckon it generally takes about 21 days for the mind to believe something, so you should see the difference after this time.

Practise gratitude

I have found this to be incredibly helpful. I have covered it in chapter 6, so I will only mention it here. The more grateful you are for the things in your life, the more you will attract better things into it. And however bad you think your life is, there is always something to be grateful for. In fact, there are a lot of things to be grateful for, if you really stop to think about them.

Service to others

When you do things for others, it gives you a great deal of satisfaction. Eventually, you realise that giving is far more rewarding than receiving. It will make you much happier.

It is my dream to become a good enough healer and animal communicator that I can volunteer at animal rescue centres. Being able to help animals in this way would give me far more satisfaction and happiness than winning the lottery. This is what I am working towards. Having an aim and purpose in life is so important at any age. It sustains you and encourages you to grow. Watch this space!

Read empowering books

I feel that the spiritual books I have read have contributed enormously to my journey. Not only have I learned an awful lot, but some of those books have been so loving and heart opening, that they do increase your vibration. They also add enormously to your feeling of positivity. Some of these authors are so inspiring. Many have gone through some of the worst ordeals and situations than you can possibly imagine; they have hit absolute rock-bottom, yet through their spiritual experiences they have risen like the phoenix from the ashes, and have become some of the best teachers and healers you could come across. They lead by example.

Avoid the media

The last couple of years I have avoided the news as much as possible, and now watch very little television. I think the media paints a very one-sided picture; they create a lot of fear and there are few heart-warming stories. Some people may feel that this is just burying your head in the sand, and that it is important to keep up to date with what is going on in the world. But I don't agree. I refuse to get sucked into the negative thinking that the media portrays, and I know I keep my vibration higher by avoiding it.

The power of prayer

This is a massive spiritual tool and most people are unaware of how powerful an effect it can have. Although we are taught The Lord's prayer at school, we are not really taught how to pray. Most of us just chant mindlessly, using it as an excuse to daydream. But, when done properly, praying can have a massive impact.

I believe that I am where I am today, because of a prayer. Five years ago, my prayer was made, passionately from the heart. "If there is a way to communicate and talk to animals can you please show me it." I now believe that because this was in line with my soul purpose, my prayer was answered. Just two weeks later, someone on the yard asked me what I thought about animal communication. It transpired that a communication had been carried out on her horse; the woman who carried it out, had communicated telepathically with her horse from a photograph, and had relayed the information back to my friend through a telephone conversation. My friend found it remarkably accurate. I had not really heard of this before, so went home and googled it. I was amazed to find out that this was a skill, it was claimed, we all had the ability to perfect, and you could even obtain a diploma in it. Coming so soon after my prayer, I knew this was a path that was being shown to me, as a way of realising my dream. I was in awe. And hooked! I suddenly became addicted to reading again; but only books on animal communication. I believe that those books opened my heart and mind to such an extent, that when Tiffany died, I was open enough to witness all the beautiful things that were happening. It was the start of an incredible journey.

Since then, I have used prayer regularly, and I always feel my prayers are answered. There are a few stories in this book, which arose from a prayer, so I won't repeat them again. Mostly, I ask to be a channel for love and healing, and to be guided down the path that is right for me. I am so happy how far I have come, and definitely feel guided. The right people and opportunities have come into my life, and the timing has been perfect; for me, there is no doubt that my prayers have been answered.

Sometimes, the power of prayer can produce a miracle; particularly, when a few people are praying for the same thing. There is a story that my dad loves telling me, which left him in no doubt whatsoever that prayer can be a very powerful instrument indeed. This is the story told in my dad's own words:-

I was a teenage student studying at the local university, and on this particular night I remember being in the kitchen with my mother, when my father came home from work. He was Assistant to the chief works engineer, and on entering the kitchen, he told us that his boss had been called to the hospital where his young son had been in for some time as a patient. I can't remember what was wrong with him; it may even have been something the hospital wasn't sure about. But evidently the doctors didn't expect the lad to last the night; hence the call for his dad to go to the hospital. Normally before going to bed, we would kneel at the bedside and say our prayers. This particular night it was cold, so the three of us knelt at the same time in the warm lounge, as the embers from the fire were dying away.

The following evening, mum and I were in the kitchen again when dad arrived home. Mum immediately asked about the son of dad's boss. Was he still alive and was there any news? I well remember my dad's response. "Ha! It is very interesting!" Apparently his boss had been at work and recounted his story of the night before. He had been by his son's bedside holding his hand and feeling the life ebbing out of him, when suddenly and inexplicably the strangest thing had happened. The life seemed to flow back into him and miraculously he suddenly perked up. The doctors were amazed at this sudden turn around, believing that he would go on to make a full recovery, which he did. My dad asked what time this happened. His boss told him that he had actually looked at his watch, so he was able to give him the precise time. Then my father said, "You know, that was the time we were saying our prayers and I prayed for him." My mum and I admitted that we had also been praying for him. If ever there was a clearer sign of prayers been answered, this was it. "Did you tell him about our prayers?" Mum asked. Dad replied that he hadn't felt it appropriate to say anything. His boss was an atheist and he often pulled dad's leg about being a Christian. But he did promise to tell him at some point; when the time was right.

Sadly, I never asked my dad whether he ever told him the full story. I wish I had, because it would have been interesting to have known his reaction. Would it have altered his attitude towards God and prayer?

That man may have been unaware that a prayer had been answered, but my dad was very much aware, and prayer has remained very important and significant in his life. In the first chapter, I recounted another story, where through prayer my dad not only felt his prayers were answered; he actually believed he heard God speaking directly to him.

It is a shame that so few people recognise the power of prayer. Or, they think that their prayer was unanswered because they didn't get what they asked for. But the thing is, prayer doesn't work that way. It isn't a magic wand. So for example, if someone is dying, and we pray for them to live, they may still die anyway, because it may be that is what is best for them, or it may be their time to die. However, if we pray for something that is in line with our soul purpose or evolution, then we are more likely to see results, although it doesn't always come in a form that we are anticipating. But it will come to us in a way that is beneficial to our soul; as opposed to our ego.

My advice is, don't be afraid to use prayer as a means of help and don't feel guilty about it either. Pray from the heart, and don't doubt for a minute that it will be answered. Have faith. Finally, be thankful and be grateful for whatever you get; know it is for your highest good.

Reiki

Reiki has been a massive tool in my spiritual development and it has really helped me grow. Additionally, I have found it amazing in warding off illnesses, or dealing with pain such as headaches or back pain. I have used it hundreds of times, and I always see results.

Reiki is a system of energy healing which originated from Japan. It is based on the belief that life energy flows through all living things. When this energy becomes disrupted or blocked, it is believed that stress and disease follow. Reiki practitioners use the Universal life energy they have been attuned to, to promote natural healing. The attunement involves a Reiki master who acts as a mirror, to help the student adjust to the energy. This creates a channel between the practitioner and the universal life energy, so they can access and use the energy to help others. Using hands, Reiki practitioners use the energy to help balance the client's energy and promote healing.

I have been attuned to Reiki at master level. My intention was to use it to help heal horses, but in truth, Reiki has been a massive tool in my own healing. Until I took the Reiki path, I hadn't realised how many blockages I had, and how limited my thinking had become. Looking how far I have come, I realise that this holistic practice has been a massive personal development tool for my mind, spirit and body. It has really helped transform me into the person I am today. I am so very grateful for this healing energy, and for having it in my life.

There are so many ways you can use Reiki. One of the more unusual was to help my horse accept her stable. On our yard, the horses have to be brought into the stables at night, from 1st November. Jazz had never been totally comfortable in her stable, often box-walking and weaving (a stress response). The evening I had to bring her in, I spent 30 minutes energetically clearing her stable. I filled the stable with Reiki energy, and put some of the Reiki symbols (not literally) on all four walls of the stable. When I led my horse in, she just went straight to her feed, and after polishing that off, she went straight to her haynet. Her response absolutely amazed me. I thought I may have to carry out this exercise periodically, but it proved not to be necessary. My horse remained calm in her stable throughout the winter, even when the horse next door left for another yard, and the stable was left empty for a couple of weeks. For my horse, this was nothing short of miraculous.

I would love everyone to have the gift of Reiki in their lives.

Animal Communication (AC)

As well as Reiki, learning animal communication has brought me incredible joy. Sometimes, I can't quite believe how miraculous it all is. I feel so blessed to have found these practices, and to be using them to such great effect in my life.

Animal communication works in a similar way to Reiki. As mentioned above, it is based on the idea that life energy flows through all living things. With

AC, you are tuning into the life force energy of a particular animal, a bit like tuning into the frequency of a radio transmitter. Once you are tuned in, you can communicate telepathically with the animal, asking questions and receiving answers. I see pictures in my third eye, as well as feeling things physically in my body that the animal is transferring to me, and I also hear them telling me things. I believe that the Universe translates what the animal wants to say into a language we can understand and pick up. Sometimes I also hear a song in my head, or a title of a song comes to me, and when I read the lyrics, it ties in with what the animal has been saying.

Strangely enough, I find it easier working from a photograph of an animal, than actually being in the presence of the animal. This may be because working at home, it is easier to focus and enter the light trance that is necessary for this type of work. It does take a while to actually believe that you are really doing this amazing work, and you aren't just making it up in your mind. When I connect with an animal, things flow so easily and naturally. Some animals talk so fast that it is hard to keep up; some are very humorous, and some are philosophical. I have learned to accept that this is really happening, due to the emotional feedback I get from the owner, and the fact that in spite of talking to so many dogs, cats and horses, every communication is very different. None have been at all similar. I believe that if it was my mind making it up, then they would all be very much along the same lines. And with every animal, there are always some very specific details, which the owner has confirmed as being correct

I believe through AC, that I connect with the animal's beautiful soul. When I do this work, I always feel that I am taken somewhere wondrous and pure. After I have finished, I always feel incredibly blessed and privileged that the animal has allowed me to connect with their soul in this way. A few times, I have been really fortunate to have met the animal I have communicated with. They always seem so very grateful towards me. The horses kiss me all over my face, and a dog whom I had communicated with, tried to lick me on my face, much to the amazement of the owner, who claimed that he wouldn't even do that to her, as normally he hates people putting their face close to his.

I know this sounds incredibly far-fetched, but I would urge you all to check out a 50 minute documentary on Youtube, which is probably one of the best documentaries I have ever seen. It features Anna Breytenbach, a South African communicator. There is some breathtaking footage, particularly with a black leopard she communicates with. Accompanying her, are a conservationist journalist and a scientist, and although sceptical at the beginning, they are both totally convinced of her talents by the end. The scientist makes a very valid point; a few hundred years ago, people didn't understand electricity like they do today. To them, it would have been paranormal. So perhaps AC is the same kind of thing and in a100 years or so, it will be entirely normal to communicate with animals this way. There are just things at work that we don't fully understand yet.

If you are still unconvinced, then go try it. You should never criticise anything, until you have explored it and tried it out for yourself. There are a lot of courses available. I did two online courses, and they were both brilliant. By the end of the course, everyone felt they had some ability to do it, and a few of them have now gone on to set up businesses carrying out this work.

Tarot or oracle cards

One of the easiest ways to connect to the divine and get messages is through tarot or oracle card readings. I have a pack of horse cards ("The way of the horse" produced by Linda Kohanav) which I used throughout my Reiki 2 assignments. It seemed appropriate to use these cards, as most of my case studies were with horses. Although I had never done card readings before, I found these cards incredibly insightful, and I was quite blown away by the information that was being revealed to me. I have since gone on to purchase a few other packs, and I love the guidance these bring.

With card reading, you can keep it simple. I often ask "What do I need to know at this time?" and ask for a card that will give me this information. Sometimes more than one card drops out, and sometimes these cards need to be read together, to give a complete answer. The once, when using the horse cards, I had asked for one card, but two dropped out. I reshuffled them, and the same two dropped out. I reshuffled them again, and still the same two dropped out. I couldn't believe it! The odds on this happening would be quite ridiculous. By this time, I realised that the two cards needed to be read together. They both related to dance, picturing a woman dancing with a horse, and in fact, when I checked the rest of the deck, they were the only two cards in the pack that had this dance theme. I also understood the meaning of the cards in relation to the question I had asked, and also realised that each of them on their own would have only have given me half the answer. The two cards together made perfect sense, giving me a much more comprehensive and understandable answer.

Finally, it is important to stress that we are all unique individuals, so although these tools have all been of massive benefit to me, this may not be the case with you. Take the time
to consider whether any of these things really resonate with you, and if they don't, then take the time to discover what does. There are literally hundreds, if not thousands, of self-help tools out

there, all which are beneficial. It is just a case of exploring and experimenting, until you find ones that work for you, creating an energy space that will allow you to be at your happiest and healthiest.

CHAPTER 16   THE FUTURE

A distant memory stirs within
Of times long gone -before our "sin"
 When once our fields were full of life
Singing skylarks soothed our strife.
Flowers danced to the wind's strong beat
 Showering petals at our feet.
Vibrant colours reigned supreme,
Summoned now briefly in a dream.

Man had choice, but took no heed
Of warnings clear, to curb his greed
Planet choked by his demands
Fields replaced by swathes of sand.
The button was pressed to "self destruct"
From his grasp, heaven was plucked.

Reality now forever dark,
Melted glaciers have left their mark.
The spectre waves his malevolent hand,
Sprinkling seeds of decay across the land.
Long gone the smell of sweet perfume,
The scent of death now spells our doom.

I can't normally write poetry to save my life, but this poem came through effortlessly and quickly, as we were travelling to our holiday destination. Unusually for me, it is very dark and depressing; definitely not the sort of thing I have ever written about before. I believe it was channelled. And I also believe it is a warning; that if we don't change our ways, then this is where we are heading.

Things aren't looking good at the moment. Two hundred years ago, there were 1 billion people on the planet; there are now 7 billion. As the population increases, so does our demands for the resources on planet earth. As I am writing this, there is depressing news coming through. The global population of wild animals has declined 60% since 1970, and it is estimated that we will have lost two-thirds of wild animals by 2020. It goes without saying that if we lose biodiversity and the natural world, then the life support systems as we know them will collapse. We are on the road to mass extinction, according to various reports.

We live on an incredibly beautiful planet, yet our greed and the rise of the corporate entity, with its "profit at all costs" attitude is threatening our future. More and more animals are becoming extinct, and with the loss of trees and forests, and land, this is going to happen at a faster rate. A big problem, and which many fail to see, is that our eco-systems are very precariously balanced. All life – be it plant or animal – is dependent on each other, and needs to co-exist alongside each other, for survival. There needs to be the right balance, and without this, problems start to arise. Climate change is only going to exacerbate things further.

But climate change isn't the only problem. In our country, we have very little industry and everything is becoming more and more automated. I do wonder how future generations will be employed, when robots and computers will have taken on so many roles. What opportunities will people have to make money? How will they survive?

On top of this, there are the problems of war, conflict and terrorism. Humans may be regarded as the most intelligent of all the animals, but we are also the most aggressive and destructive. As I write this, I have just seen an article written by the great physicist, Stephen Hawking, who seems to have the same opinions as me. He writes

Now, more than at any time in our history, our species needs to work together. We face awesome environmental challenges; climate change, food production, overpopulation, the decimation of other species, epidemic disease, acidification of the ocean. Together they are a reminder that we are at the most dangerous moment in the development of humanity. We now have the technology to destroy the planet on which we live, but we have not yet developed the ability to escape it. Perhaps in a few hundred years, we will have established human colonies amid the stars, but right now we only have one planet, and we need to work together to protect it.

Our very planet is threatened by our behaviour. If the destruction is to be reversed, then we need to change. And this change has to start with the way we think and interact with everything around us. We all need to recognise that each and every one of us has a part to play in the future of the planet. It is essential that we all awaken to our responsibility to mother earth, and adopt a more loving and healing attitude to nature and to each other. Most spiritual thinking is based on the idea that this can only be achieved by us all raising our consciousness, and many believe that this is already happening. The rest of the chapter is devoted to exploring the main spiritual ideas relating to the changes that are perceived to be taking place, and the steps that need to be taken to ensure the survival of the planet. The ideas that I present to you may sound absolutely crazy, but my own experience has transformed the way I view reality, so for me, it doesn't seem as implausible as it may first appear.

The new consciousness

The date 21 December 2012 was considered so significant, that even the media got caught up in the frenzy. This date was to do with the Mayan prophecy. The media was reporting that the Mayans had predicted that this date would mark the end of the world. As the world waited to see whether the prediction would unfold, the more spiritual amongst us just despaired that the prophecy had been so misinterpreted. Once again, the media were using scare tactics to sell newspapers!

In spiritual circles, the interpretation of the prophecy was very different. The date did not mark the end of the world; it marked the change in our level of consciousness. The Mayans believed that from that date, the vibrations in the world would increase, and more and more people would start to awaken. Eventually, the number of awakened people would reach "critical mass" and from this point the world can start to emerge from a 3D reality into a 4th and eventually a fifth dimensional reality. But, this was never going to happen overnight; it is a process that is expected to take decades to achieve. Our perception of reality is altered by whichever dimension our consciousness is currently residing in. This is not fixed, and so we will move between the different dimensions.

Different dimensions

Dimensions are levels of consciousness that vibrate at a certain rate. Each dimension vibrates at a higher rate than the one below. Generally, in each higher dimension, there exists a clearer, wider perspective of reality; a greater level of knowing. We experience more freedom, greater power, and more opportunity to create reality. In order for a higher dimension to be available to us, we need to vibrate in resonance with it.

The 3rd dimension

This is the traditional state of consciousness, and a lot of people are still in this dimension, although more and more are feeling the pull into the 4th. In this state, consciousness is very limited and restricted. Everything is subject to gravity, and physical objects appear solid. There is a belief in duality, and fear and judgement are pervasive.

The 4th dimension

In this dimension, there are moments of spiritual awakening, and experiences of heart opening. Everything around us feels lighter and less rigid. We feel more joy, love and gratitude. Time is no longer linear. There's an ongoing sense of being in the present time, with no interest or awareness of past and future. And we can discover that time is malleable – it can actually stretch and condense. Manifestation is much faster. Something we think about can show up very quickly.

The 5th dimension

This is the dimension of love; of living totally from the heart. In this dimension, there is no fear, anger, hostility, guilt, suffering or sense of separation. Manifestation is instantaneous. People can read other people's thoughts with ease. The experience of time is radically different – "everything is happening at once", and there is no distinction between past, present and future. To be in this dimension, mastery over thought is a pre-requisite.

Transitional times

When people start to transition from one dimension to another, it will often come with some chaos, confusion and disorientation. This is because whatever does not serve you, in shifting to a higher dimension, has to fall away. This means that there could be radical changes in your life. You may need to change jobs, or move to another area. There may be some friends who no longer resonate with you, and so you lose their friendship. Conversely, new people will come into your life who do resonate with you.

The world itself is also believed to be currently transitioning from the 3rd to the 4th dimension. It is for this reason that our current systems and structures are breaking down. A lot of fears are being brought to the surface, and people are aware that change is needed. Reality as we knew it is unravelling. There will be more chaos and confusion as the old systems and ways of being, crumble. This will then allow for the new to come in.

A fifth dimensional world

If enough people graduate to the fifth dimensional reality, then in time, the world itself will exist in a fifth dimension. In this reality, all people will live in peace and harmony, experiencing oneness with all life. Love and compassion will flow through all communications. There will be complete equality, justice and respect for all human beings, and everything and everyone will be seen as equal. There will be no hunger, poverty or crime, because we will all be looking after each other, and recognising that there is enough abundance in the world for everyone. Fear will be a thing of the past, as we will have complete trust in the divine, and we will recognise this reality for what it truly is. Everyone will be awake to the majestic, divine, inter-dimensional beings they truly are.

Now I don't know about you, but this is a world I would truly enjoy living in.

New wave volunteers

This thinking is certainly backed up by others in their field of expertise. Dolores Cannon was a hypnotherapist, who specialised in past life regression. Her career spanned 50 years. In addition she wrote a large volume of books on the subject. She developed a unique method of hypnosis known as the "Quantum Healing Hypnosis Technique (QHHT)" which took clients into a much deeper level of hypnosis than was previously achieved. In this state, her clients were effortlessly able to relive past lives. But the interesting thing about her work is that in the last decade of her life, she started to come across something completely unique in the people she was regressing; whereas previously, people were describing multiple past lives on Earth, she was starting to come across more and more people who were living their first life here on Earth, and had no past life experience (on earth). These higher vibrational beings had come from other, more advanced star systems or dimensions. The sessions revealed that these new wave volunteers had chosen to come to Earth at this specific time, with the intention of helping humanity raise its vibration in the process of ascension. They possess the knowledge and wisdom that will help humanity complete the transition to the 5th dimensional reality.

Dolores was able to identify three types of volunteers. She also discovered that they were often diagnosed with ADD, ADHD or they were on the autistic spectrum. Their special abilities are misunderstood, and medication is seen as the answer to their differences, by a world that doesn't understand. Hopefully, in the future, we will start to recognise the abilities these people have, and realise we need to learn from them. On one of my spiritual courses I attended, I came across a lady whose son was autistic. She told me that she viewed his autism as a gift, and because his perception of reality was so different, she had learned an awful lot from him. She felt he had advanced her own thinking by really opening her mind to new possibilities.

Interestingly, another writer, Doreen Virtue, makes very similar observations to Dolores, but from a very different angle. Doreen holds a BA, MA and PHD in counselling psychology, and is a lifelong clairvoyant, who works with the angelic realm. She has written a large volume of books, and is highly regarded and respected in her field. She also identified three waves of volunteers, who she termed the indigo, crystal and rainbow children. As with Dolores, she classified them into age ranges and different abilities, and also identified many as having ADHD or being on the autistic spectrum. Again, she cites them as coming to Earth in order to raise the energy and avoid catastrophe.

Whether this is true or not, we certainly need something coming to Earth, to help save us from ourselves. The question is, have we crossed the tipping point or is there still hope we can be saved? As I am ever the optimist, I will choose the latter, although I do think we all have a part to play in saving the planet. And in my opinion, change can only come about by each of us playing our part. To do this, I think each and every one of us needs to take the path to a higher consciousness. We need to look at how we treat the earth and everyone (people, animals, plants, trees etc) on it. And we need to start acting from the highest integrity, having total respect and regard to all life forms. When we look at things from this vantage point, it is obvious that so much needs to change. First and foremost, we need to stop thinking in terms of profits, and more in terms of love, compassion and care for all life forms. We need to recognise our connection; not just to each other, but to everything.

Our future according to the angels

In her book, "Stairway to Heaven" Lorna Byrne, who has been able to communicate with angels since she was a child, is shown various futures for mankind. Which one becomes reality, is dependent on the decisions mankind makes.

One future is the path we are currently on. That is a pretty grim pathway. After destroying and plundering our planet, we go on to do the same with other planets. Man continues following his destructive tendencies and uses his scientific and technological advances to overstep the boundaries; using knowledge for the sake of power and control over others. In one such horrifying vision, Lorna is shown a human throwback; a lot of his brain and mind had been taken away, to be replaced by implants; half robot and half man. His soul was intact, but this only made the vision more horrific, as that soul was screaming in agony at what had been done to him. This vision haunted Lorna for a long time afterwards.

If however, we respond to the invitation to adopt a higher consciousness, we can save ourselves. In this future, she describes how children will be crying over their history books at the children of the past. These children won't need gadgets or technology. Instead they will be full of wonder for the world around them, and this will give them hearts full of fun and joy. They will look at a blade of grass, or an insect and see so much more than the children of today do. They will be fascinated by life, nature and everything around them, and they will love to learn.

Skills such as telepathy will be more commonplace, particularly amongst connected family members. With my experiences of telepathy, I already know this to be a reality. I also know one mother who does connect to her daughter through telepathy; they rarely use the phone. They even arrange shopping trips after school through this method.

Countries and religions will come together under one umbrella, but each country will still keep its own individuality and traditions. And traditional medicine and healing will also be unified. There is the potential for us to become so evolved that physically everyone will be perfect. Our bodies will not succumb to sickness or wear and tear. Again, there are already signs of this happening. Julie Renee is a quantum healer, who claims to be able to completely regenerate new cells. She healed herself from horrific and terminal cancer, through the re-generation process, and ever since she has been training others to do the same. She has a huge following, and thousands claim to have used her techniques successfully.

In this beautiful future, we will all be more aware of and connected to our Guardian Angel, who will become a friend, assisting us through life. Again, my experiences have taught me that this is already happening, and more and more of us are coming to this realisation.

We will travel to other planets – not to plunder them, but to connect lovingly with the people living on them, and it will be for the purpose of our evolution and theirs' also.

At a certain stage in evolution, people will not die. We will have a perfect body, which will be more like our soul. The two will be intertwined. This body and soul, having united, will go to heaven together. Life on earth will increasingly start to replicate heaven.

Lorna concludes by saying that if we evolve in the way God chooses for us, each and every one of us as a part to play. We all have to be committed to this vision of heaven on earth.

Interestingly, this positive vision of the future is very much in line with the higher consciousness theory put out by the spiritual thinkers. I like to think positively, and want to end this chapter on an optimistic note, but I do think one thing is for sure and it seems to be something that everyone agrees on. We are at a critical point in the history of humanity; the decisions we make now are critical to our future; and this is not just decisions made by world leaders. Each and every one of us has a part to play in the future of the world. Do we respond to the call asking us to evolve to a higher consciousness and create heaven on earth, or do we stagnate and risk destroying the planet? The choice is yours!

CHAPTER 17 YOUR LIFE, YOUR DREAM

Impossible is just a big word thrown around by small men who find it easier to live in the world they've been given than to explore the power they have to change it.

Muhammad Ali

Just when I thought my book was complete, and I was in the process of editing, I suddenly woke one morning with an idea for a final chapter. The title and contents were reverberating around my head. Everything that has come before is the preparation for this final message.

When we are young, most of us dream how our life is going to be. We imagine the careers we will have, the ambitions we will fulfil and the places we will visit, and some dream of the difference and impact they will make on the world. As we grow, the dreams get put aside. They start to seem unrealistic and we come up with all manner of excuses for not being able to achieve them – lack of money, experience, contacts, know-how, training etc. There is always some obstacle in the way to stop us fulfilling our dreams.

When my daughter was four years old, she stated categorically that she wanted to become an equine vet. I am ashamed to admit it now, but I was extremely negative, basically telling her it was an impossible dream. I pointed out that this was the hardest career to get into – the competition to get a university place is fierce, and you need to be an A grade student. Thankfully, the more I tried to put my daughter off the idea, the more determined she was to follow this career. It was so clearly her soul calling, as she has never wavered in her determination to walk this path, and her love, compassion and empathy with animals is beyond doubt. The last few years I have fully supported her, arranging her work experience, ferrying her around on her placements, and helping her to concoct a good Personal Statement. The effort has paid off and she commenced her veterinary degree in September 2017. I am so proud of her for never giving up on her dream.

I have learned something very valuable, and it is this: if you have a dream that you are desperate to fulfil, and that dream is beneficial either to your soul purpose, or for the benefit of others, then the Universe will do everything to support you towards your goal; leading to ways you can finance it, and bringing the opportunities and influences into your space. You need to put aside all the barriers that your mind is creating, to fulfil that dream. Don't worry about lack of money, or any of the other perceived problems – the universe will find a way around them. Just trust and have faith, and believe it is possible. If you read through the steps in the chapter on "Law of Attraction", you can put those in operation to draw your dreams to you.

This doesn't mean to say that the dream will land on your lap. It will still require a huge effort on your part to bring it into realisation, but if you are determined enough, the Universe will conspire to help you. I now believe that no dream is out of bounds; as long as it is beneficial to your soul, as opposed to your ego. I have read the most amazing accounts over the last few years, of people who have achieved the seemingly impossible and I now recognise that the only limitations are in our minds. I wanted to finish this chapter with one such story, so have decided to tell the incredible story of Stuart Sharp. His dream seemed so impossible and deluded, yet against all the odds, it was brought into his reality. This is his story.

Stuart Sharp

Stuart was married with a young daughter, but tragedy struck when his young son was born stillborn. His wife also suffered complications following the birth, and had to have several life saving operations. Despite being an atheist, on the night of his son's burial, heartbroken Stuart received a vision. In his dream, he was at his son's graveside, staring down at his white coffin. He heard distant angelic music with choirs, violins, cellos, horns and harps that grew in intensity, resembling a symphony. As he listened to the music, he saw his son's spirit rise through the coffin, and get taken to heaven by the angels. It was a deeply comforting dream, and he was mesmerised by the music.

Stuart tried to continue his life as a chef, but he was haunted by the mesmerising music. He continued to hear it on an almost daily basis until he could identify each instrument and every note. He became obsessed with composing it, even though he couldn't even read music, let alone write it. He couldn't even play an instrument.

A year of trying to continue living a normal life, Stuart fell into a deep depression. His dream had become an obsession and he could think of nothing else. He wanted to compose the music, and he wanted the Philharmonic orchestra to play it. It seemed an impossible task, but eventually Stuart knew he had to leave his family and at least try – otherwise it would destroy him. His wife, considering him completely deluded, divorced him and remarried.

So, he moved to London, but he soon became homeless. He bought an old guitar, very cheaply. In a strange twist, he bought it from a shop owned by Pete Townshend's (The Who) parents. Strangely,

Pete also had a vision when he was eleven, of an angelic orchestra – a very similar vision to the one that Stuart had experienced.

Stuart taught himself to play the guitar and recorded the haunting melody on an old tape recorder at a homeless hostel. One day as he was sitting strumming his guitar outside the BBC television centre in London, a jazz pianist, Anthony Wade, stopped to chat to him. He offered him accommodation for a while, and when he listened to the tape, he knew it was a masterpiece. Speaking bluntly, his advice was for Stuart to amass a lot of money – he would need hundreds of thousands of pounds if he was to compose the symphony and arrange for the Philharmonic orchestra to play it.

Stuart took his advice, and for the next 15 years, he worked flat out to raise the money. Through gruelling work without a break, and lots of luck, he finally got the money together. He approached Wade, and they spent the next five years creating the demo. He stood firm in his decision that only the Philharmonic orchestra would record his music, even though such an undertaking is usually reserved for film and music moguls, or firmly established composers.

Conductor, Allan Willson has described in newspapers, how the demo tape lay on his desk for a number of weeks, before he listened to it. When he did, he just couldn't believe it. He is quoted as saying, "The piece was so full of anguish, pain and intense musical passion, that I felt I was looking directly into the man's heart."

At the recording, the entire orchestra of nearly 80 musicians gave Stuart a huge, heartfelt round of applause. Such an ovation is extremely rare. The Angeli symphony was performed twenty years after his son's death and was recognised as a work of genius. Stuart has gone on to write another three symphonies, a theme song, and a further thirty pieces. He describes them as "gifts to share." He used his success to set up projects for the blind and disabled in Africa, and he is also Patron of the Canaan Trust in Nottingham, which looks after many homeless people. Recently, producers in LA have contacted him with a view to turning his story into a cinema movie and Gold Circle Films have put the film into development.

If this was a work of fiction, people would be damming it for being extremely far-fetched. It seems an impossible dream for a man who was a penniless non-musician, living in a hostel for the homeless, to not only compose a great symphony, but also to have it played by a world class orchestra. But this is the point. Where there is a will, there is a way, although there is no denying that Stuart had to make huge personal sacrifices to accomplish his dream. But that was his choice and the rewards for him were great. He describes the joy he felt when he heard the orchestra playing his symphony, as it was exactly as it sounded when he first heard it in heaven. He felt he was with the angels again. It was the culmination of his life-long purpose, and for him, there was no greater reward.

This story proves that nothing is insurmountable. If you want something badly enough, then with the right mind and thinking, it can be achieved. Your dreams are just there in your head, waiting to be turned into your reality. So, dream big and let all barriers be dissolved.

AFTERWORD

"Every great dream begins with a dreamer. Always remember, you have within you the strength, the patience, and the passion to reach for the stars to change the world."

Harriet Tubman

I hope that this book has opened your eyes to a different way of seeing, and it has given you the incentive to go on your own inner journey. I can't stress enough, that it will be unlike any path you have travelled before. Don't fixate on the destination. The journey is more important. I promise you this – you will get out of it the same as what you put in. The deeper you go, the more magical and exciting it will become. Your idea of reality will change completely, and this alone will prove to you that reality is not fixed. It changes according to your thoughts. Remember, YOU MAKE YOUR OWN REALITY.

Do not pass judgement on other people. It is not their fault we have been brought up in such a conditioning society. Just be patient and recognise that everyone is on a soul journey. Each person is where they need to be at this particular time. Some people have had more lifetimes to evolve than others, but all will get there in the time that is right for them.

The most important question to ask is, "why wouldn't I want to change my way of thinking if it could make me happier?" If you always think or do the same things, you will always get the same results. Something has to change, in order to get a different result. As everything derives from thought, then this is the biggest life changer.

Recently, a friend related a dream. She kept waking up and slipping back into the same dream. In the dream, her workmates cut off her hands and feet, and sewed up her mouth, telling her, "That will stop you!" She felt no fear or concern as to what they were doing to her – only acceptance. This dream is a brilliant metaphor as to what is happening to all of us. Society has stripped us of our power and our authentic voice, disabling us and making us ineffective. And we just accept it. We are all born as unique, perfect and magnificent beings – powerful beyond our wildest dreams, but as we grow, our imagination and creativity get sucked out of us, and our beautiful hearts become hardened and hidden. We tell ourselves that this is life. We have to take these measures in order to survive and operate effectively in the world. But all we do is cut ourselves off from the divine light that is in each and everyone, as well as all around us. In doing this, we wither and die; physical or mental illness becomes commonplace, and we believe that this is normal and real. That it is a cruel and punishing world against which we have no defence.

This is no longer my reality and it need not be yours. Each day we awaken, we have an opportunity to start anew – to live in the present moment; to draw a line under the past, and to let the future just be. Choosing love over fear will help you surrender to the present moment. I have stopped worrying over the future, as I now have complete trust in the Universe. Things will unfold as they are meant to. This doesn't mean it will always be sweetness and light. And it doesn't mean that things will always work out the way I want them to. But from a soul level point of view, I can view those moments of suffering in a more enlightened way. I can look at them objectively and ask "What lesson is there here for me?" Or recognise, as I did with the death of my horse, that if I open my heart and mind to it, then I may be able to recognise the gifts and miracles contained within that suffering.

At a sub-conscious level, we all have a deep understanding of the power within us. Take some of the most popular films. In Star Wars, we learn that "The force lies within." In Wizard of Oz, Dorothy spends most of her time searching for the Great Wizard, who will take her back home, only to discover in the end that he was just an illusion; there was no Great Wizard. Glinda the witch reveals that the power resided within Dorothy all along. "You've always had the power my dear, you just had to learn it for yourself." This is so typical of us humans. We look outside ourselves for all the answers, believing all our dreams can be met by what is out there. But the truth is this: Only we hold the power. Only we can change our lives for the better. Marianne Wilson points to the extent of this power, when she says:-

Our deepest fear is not that we are inadequate. Our deepest fear is that we are powerful beyond measure. It is our light, not our darkness that most frightens us. We ask ourselves "who am I to be brilliant, gorgeous, talented, fabulous?" Actually, who are you not to be? You are a child of God. Your playing small does not serve the world. There is nothing enlightened about shrinking so that other people won't feel insecure around you. We are all meant to shine, as children do. We were born to make manifest the glory of God that is within us. It's not just in some of us; it's in everyone. And as we let our own light shine, we unconsciously give other people permission to do the same. As we are liberated from our own fear, our presence automatically liberates others.

Thank you to those of you who have made it to the end of this book. Even though you may not agree with all my ideas, or even any of my ideas, you have at least taken the time to consider someone else's perspective. If we all did this, it would make for a more peaceful and loving world. Blessings and love to each and every one of you. Good luck on your journey and make it the most exciting one ever.

Printed in Great Britain
by Amazon